TOUCHPOINTS FOR COUPLES
God's Answers for Your Daily Needs

TouchPoints
for Couples

GOD'S ANSWERS FOR
YOUR DAILY NEEDS

Tyndale House Publishers, Inc.
Wheaton, Illinois

Visit Tyndale's exciting Web site at www.tyndale.com

General editors: Ronald A. Beers and V. Gilbert Beers

Scripture selection and compilation by Rhonda K. O'Brien

Contributing writers: Rhonda K. O'Brien, Douglas J. Rumford, V. Gilbert Beers, Ronald A. Beers, Shawn A. Harrison, Jonathan Gray, and Brian R. Coffey.

Tyndale House editor: Shawn A. Harrison

ISBN 0-8423-4226-5

Printed in the United States of America

07 06 05 04 03 02 01 00
10 9 8 7 5 3 2 1

PREFACE

*Psalm 119:111, 162 Your decrees are my
treasure; they are truly my heart's delight. . . . I rejoice
in your word like one who finds a great treasure.*

*Psalm 119:91, 160 Your laws remain true
today, for everything serves your plans. . . . All your
words are true; all your just laws will stand forever.*

*Psalm 119:105 Your word is a lamp for my feet
and a light for my path.*

What a treasure we have in God's word! The Holy
Bible is relevant to today's issues and gives solid
guidance for daily living.

In this book you will find over one hundred
topics for daily living and what the Bible says about
each one. Each topic is listed alphabetically, with
several questions, Scripture passages, and comments
addressing each topic. In the index at the back of
this book, you will find a complete listing of all the
topics for quick reference. You can read through this
book page by page or use it as a reference guide for
topics of particular interest to you.

While we could not cover all topics, questions,

and Scriptures related to the subject of this book, our prayer is that you will continue to deliberately search God's word. May you find God's answers as he longs to be your daily guide. Enjoy your treasure hunt!

THE EDITORS

2 Timothy 3:16-17 *All Scripture is inspired by God and is useful to teach us what is true and to make us realize what is wrong in our lives. It straightens us out and teaches us to do what is right. It is God's way of preparing us in every way, fully equipped for every good thing God wants us to do.*

Absence

Why is it important for us not to be absent in our relationships?

Ecclesiastes 4:9-10 *Two people can accomplish more than twice as much as one; they get a better return for their labor. If one person falls, the other can reach out and help. But people who are alone when they fall are in real trouble.*
Our presence provides physical support to another. Two can form a team and accomplish much more together than separately.

Job 42:11 *Then all his brothers, sisters, and former friends came and feasted with him in his home. And they consoled him and comforted him because of all the trials the LORD had brought against him.*

Genesis 45:15 *Then Joseph kissed each of his brothers and wept over them, and then they began talking freely with him.*

2 Corinthians 7:6 *But God, who encourages those who are discouraged, encouraged us by the arrival of Titus.*
Our presence provides emotional support to another. When we need "a lift" emotionally, an inanimate object doesn't do much for us. It takes a smile, a kind word, a hug, a touch from someone who cares.

Psalm 34:3 *Come, let us tell of the LORD's greatness; let us exalt his name together.*

Acts 1:14 *They all met together continually for prayer.*

Hebrews 10:25 *Let us not neglect our meeting together, as some people do, but encourage and warn each other.*
Our presence provides spiritual support to another. God's people should bring others into God's presence or bring God's presence to them.

How can we compensate for those times when our physical presence is not possible?

Matthew 19:6 *Since they are no longer two but one, let no one separate them, for God has joined them together.*

1 Corinthians 5:3-4 *Even though I am not there with you in person, I am with you in the*

Spirit. . . . I will be there in spirit, and the power of the Lord Jesus will be with you.
When we are not physically present, we can still exercise our commitment to our relationship. Two caring people can provide emotional and spiritual support for each other at a distance.

Philippians 1:7 *It is right that I should feel as I do about all of you, for you have a very special place in my heart. We have shared together the blessings of God, both when I was in prison and when I was out, defending the truth and telling others the Good News.*
We can recall to mind the times we have shared together. True love does not diminish or fade with distance.

2 John 1:12 *Well, I have much more to say to you, but I don't want to say it in a letter. For I hope to visit you soon and to talk with you face to face. Then our joy will be complete.*

3 John 1:14 *For I hope to see you soon, and then we will talk face to face.*
We can communicate our desire to see the other person. Face-to-face encounters are certainly precious. But a phone call, letter, fax, or E-mail can go a long way in bringing us closer to another.

2 Timothy 1:4 *I long to see you again, for I remember your tears as we parted. And I will be filled with joy when we are together again.*

3

We can look forward to our reunion with joyful anticipation.

PROMISE FROM GOD: Ecclesiastes 4:9-10 *Two people can accomplish more than twice as much as one; they get a better return for their labor. If one person falls, the other can reach out and help. But people who are alone when they fall are in real trouble.*

Abuse

How do I heal the wounds of abuse?

Matthew 15:30 *[Jesus] healed them all.*
Jesus can truly heal broken hearts and lives.

Philippians 4:8 *Fix your thoughts on what is true and honorable and right. Think about things that are pure and lovely and admirable. Think about things that are excellent and worthy of praise.*
As we fill our minds with thoughts about God, we have less room and less time to dwell on the past.

Will God forgive a person who is guilty of abuse?

Acts 2:21 *And anyone who calls on the name of the Lord will be saved.*

Luke 23:34 *Father, forgive these people, because they don't know what they are doing.*

4

God will forgive any sin, not just certain ones. His mercy is available to anyone who calls on him, regardless of that person's past.

2 Chronicles 33:6, 12-13 *Manasseh even sacrificed his own sons in the fire in the valley of the son of Hinnom. . . . But while in deep distress, Manasseh sought the LORD his God and cried out humbly to the God of his ancestors. 13And when he prayed, the LORD listened to him and was moved by his request for help.* Manasseh was one of the most wicked kings in Judah's history, abusive to the point of killing his own sons on an altar. Later in life Manasseh sought God's forgiveness. God forgave him, transforming him into a man who did great things for his nation.

PROMISE FROM GOD: 2 Corinthians 4:9 *We are hunted down, but God never abandons us. We get knocked down, but we get up again and keep going.*

Accountability

Does God really hold us accountable for all our actions?

Ecclesiastes 11:9 *Do everything you want to do; take it all in. But remember that you must give an account to God for everything you do.*

God will hold us accountable for everything we do. So enjoy life, but remember that God is watching. Who wants to explain ungodliness to a holy God on the day of judgment?

What happens when there is no accountability?

Judges 17:6 *The people did whatever seemed right in their own eyes.*
Left unaccountable, we will always lean toward sin. The consequences of those sins will hurt not only us but also many others, including God.

How do we become more accountable?

Psalm 119:9 *How can a young person stay pure? By obeying your word and following its rules.*

Psalm 1:1 *Oh, the joys of those who do not follow the advice of the wicked.*

Proverbs 27:6 *Wounds from a friend are better than many kisses from an enemy.*
To become more accountable, follow God's commands as outlined in his word, the Bible. Choose wise friends who can counsel you and help keep you accountable.

PROMISE FROM GOD: 1 John 2:3 *How can we be sure that we belong to him? By obeying his commandments.*

Accusations

How should we respond to accusations against us?

Psalm 35:21-24 *They shout that they have seen me doing wrong. "Aha," they say. "Aha! With our own eyes we saw him do it!" O LORD, you know all about this. . . . Rise to my defense! Take up my case, my God and my Lord. Declare me "not guilty," O LORD my God, for you give justice.*
Realize that God has full knowledge of the truth and that he has the authority and ability to handle the situation.

Psalm 119:78 *Bring disgrace upon the arrogant people who lied about me; meanwhile, I will concentrate on your commandments.*

Nehemiah 6:8-9 *My reply was, "You know you are lying. There is no truth in any part of your story." They were just trying to intimidate us, imagining that they could break our resolve and stop the work. So I prayed for strength to continue the work.*
Don't become so focused on the accusation that you forget about God. Take the matter to him and get strength from him.

Genesis 3:11-13 *"Have you eaten the fruit I commanded you not to eat?" "Yes," Adam admitted, "but it was the woman you gave me who brought me* the fruit, and I ate it." Then the LORD God asked the woman, "How could you do such a thing?" "The serpent tricked me," she replied. "That's why I ate it."

Hosea 4:4 "Don't point your finger at someone else and try to pass the blame!"
There are times when we should accept the blame that is rightfully ours.

Luke 12:11-12 And when you are brought to trial in the synagogues and before rulers and authorities, don't worry about what to say in your defense, for the Holy Spirit will teach you what needs to be said even as you are standing there.
Be sensitive to the Holy Spirit's guidance in responding to accusations. He may give you help you never thought possible.

Matthew 27:12-14 But when the leading priests and other leaders made their accusations against him, Jesus remained silent. "Don't you hear their many charges against you?" Pilate demanded. But Jesus said nothing, much to the governor's great surprise.
In some instances it is best to remain silent. There are times when your silence shouts your innocence.

1 Peter 2:12, 15 Be careful how you live among your unbelieving neighbors. Even if they accuse you of doing wrong, they will see your honorable behavior, and they will believe and give honor to God when he comes to judge the world. . . . It is God's will that your good lives should silence those who make foolish accusations against you.

Live an honorable life before your accusers. Christlikeness is magnetic. You may attract the accuser to the Savior.

How do we accuse the right way?

Matthew 7:3, 5 *Why worry about a speck in your friend's eye when you have a log in your own? . . . First get rid of the log from your own eye; then perhaps you will see well enough to deal with the speck in your friend's eye.*

John 8:7 *"All right, stone her. But let those who have never sinned throw the first stones!"*
Self-examination should precede accusation. Perhaps then we will accuse ourselves of our wrongs instead of accusing others of lesser wrongs.

Leviticus 19:11 *Do not steal. Do not cheat one another. Do not lie.*

Proverbs 3:30 *Don't make accusations against someone who hasn't wronged you.*
We should never make false accusations. Accusing another falsely may cast suspicion on a person's reputation, cheating that person of something precious.

PROMISES FROM GOD: 1 Peter 3:16 *Keep your conscience clear. Then if people speak evil against you, they will be ashamed when they see what a good life you live because you belong to Christ.*

9

Colossians 1:22 *Now he has brought you back as his friends. He has done this through his death on the cross in his own human body. As a result, he has brought you into the very presence of God, and you are holy and blameless as you stand before him without a single fault.*

Adapt/Adaptable

How do we best adapt to change?

Ecclesiastes 3:11 *God has made everything beautiful for its own time. He has planted eternity in the human heart, but even so, people cannot see the whole scope of God's work from beginning to end.*

It is wise to adapt to normal cycles of change. When we recognize life's seasons, we will be more equipped to adapt to them. But in adapting to change, we are wise not to compromise changeless truths in life.

James 1:2-4 *Dear brothers and sisters, whenever trouble comes your way, let it be an opportunity for joy. For when your faith is tested, your endurance has a chance to grow. So let it grow, for when your endurance is fully developed, you will be strong in character and ready for anything.*

Times of trouble, which lead to the testing of our faith and the increasing of our endurance, help to strengthen our character and adapt to whatever the future holds. Use times of change and challenge as growing times rather than giving-up times.

Genesis 12:1 *The LORD told Abram, "Leave your country, your relatives, and your father's house, and go to the land that I will show you."*
You don't need to know all the details of God's plan for you in order to adapt to it. Sometimes adapting to God's way means moving forward in faith and obedience, realizing that since he knows the way we don't have to.

Exodus 14:15-16 *Then the LORD said to Moses, "Why are you crying out to me? Tell the people to get moving! Use your shepherd's staff—hold it out over the water, and a path will open up before you through the sea. Then all the people of Israel will walk through on dry ground."*
Sometimes we must adapt quickly. There's a time to stop and pray and a time to pray on the run.

What kinds of things should we be unwilling to adapt to?

Exodus 23:2 *Do not join a crowd that intends to do evil. When you are on the witness stand, do not be swayed in your testimony by the opinion of the majority.*

11

Ezekiel 20:32 *You say, "We want to be like the nations all around us, who serve idols of wood and stone."* We should not adapt to those around us when they are not following God's ways.

PROMISE FROM GOD: Romans 12:2 *Don't copy the behavior and customs of this world, but let God transform you into a new person by changing the way you think. Then you will know what God wants you to do, and you will know how good and pleasing and perfect his will really is.*

Admiration

What should be admirable about us?

Proverbs 31:30 *Charm is deceptive, and beauty does not last; but a woman who fears the LORD will be greatly praised.*
Honoring and respecting the Lord are admirable qualities.

Ecclesiastes 2:13 *Wisdom is of more value than foolishness, just as light is better than darkness.*

Proverbs 12:8 *Everyone admires a person with good sense, but a warped mind is despised.*
Wisdom and good sense are admirable qualities.

2 Corinthians 9:13-14 *You will be glorifying God through your generous gifts. . . . And they will*

pray for you with deep affection because of the wonderful grace of God shown through you.
Graciousness and generosity are admirable and bring glory to God.

How can I express my admiration for my spouse?

Ephesians 5:33 *So again I say, each man must love his wife as he loves himself, and the wife must respect her husband.*

Romans 12:10 *Love each other with genuine affection, and take delight in honoring each other.*
I can express my admiration for my spouse by showing him or her love, honor, respect, and affection.

Proverbs 31:28-29 *Her children stand and bless her. Her husband praises her: "There are many virtuous and capable women in the world, but you surpass them all!"*
I can express my admiration for my spouse by saying so publicly, honoring my mate to others.

Job 29:24 *When they were discouraged, I smiled at them. My look of approval was precious to them.*
Even my smile and the look on my face should show approval of and admiration for my spouse.

PROMISE FROM GOD: Philippians 4:8
Fix your thoughts on what is true and honorable and right. Think about things that are pure and lovely and admirable. Think about things that are excellent and worthy of praise.

Adultery

What is God's definition of adultery?

Hebrews 13:4 *Give honor to marriage, and remain faithful to one another in marriage. God will surely judge people who are immoral and those who commit adultery.*
Adultery is being unfaithful to your mate. Normally, this involves forming a sexual relationship with someone other than your spouse. But even an intimate emotional relationship with another can become adulterous if it takes us away from our first love. In the spiritual realm, we commit adultery against God when we are unfaithful to him by worshiping anything or anyone except him.

Mark 10:11 *He told them, "Whoever divorces his wife and marries someone else commits adultery against her."*
Remaining faithful "'til death do us part" is a serious commitment—breaking the marriage vow and joining with another is adultery.

14

Matthew 5:28 *Anyone who even looks at a woman with lust in his eye has already committed adultery with her in his heart.*
When we look at another with lust, we are being unfaithful to our spouses.

Why is it important for us not to get involved in adultery?

Exodus 20:14 *Do not commit adultery.*
God has commanded us to be faithful to our spouses.

Proverbs 6:27-29 *Can a man scoop fire into his lap and not be burned? Can he walk on hot coals and not blister his feet? So it is with the man who sleeps with another man's wife. He who embraces her will not go unpunished.*
Adultery's momentary pleasure isn't worth the consequences that it brings—a lifetime of regret and pain.

1 Corinthians 6:9-10 *Don't you know that those who do wrong will have no share in the Kingdom of God? . . . Those who indulge in sexual sin, who are . . . adulterers . . . none of these will have a share in the Kingdom of God.*
Even if our sin is not caught during our lifetime, we won't get away with it forever.

How do we protect ourselves from getting into an adulterous relationship?

Proverbs 2:16 *Wisdom will save you from the immoral woman, from the flattery of the adulterous woman.*

God promises wisdom to those who ask him for it (James 1:5). A wise person will avoid getting into adultery.

Proverbs 4:25-27 *Look straight ahead, and fix your eyes on what lies before you. Mark out a straight path for your feet; then stick to the path and stay safe. Don't get sidetracked; keep your feet from following evil.*

If looking can lead us into adultery, then not looking will help us avoid it. It can be challenging to have "faithful eyes," but they are a key to success for avoiding adultery.

Proverbs 5:3-4, 7-9 *The lips of an immoral woman are as sweet as honey, and her mouth is smoother than oil. But the result is as bitter as poison, sharp as a double-edged sword. . . . My sons, listen to me. Never stray from what I am about to say: Run from her! Don't go near the door of her house! If you do, you will lose your honor and hand over to merciless people everything you have achieved in life.*

When faced with temptation, we might be tempted to think that we can handle it, but the best course is to run away and not look back (see Gen. 39:1-20).

16

Proverbs 5:15, 18 *Drink water from your own well—share your love only with your wife. . . . Let your wife be a fountain of blessing for you. Rejoice in the wife of your youth.*

Adultery is more likely if we allow discontentment to creep into our hearts. But we can be content and satisfied with our mate. Then we won't "shop around."

PROMISE FROM GOD: Proverbs 6.24 *These commands and this teaching will keep you from the immoral woman, from the smooth tongue of an adulterous woman.*

Affection

How can I show my affection for my spouse?

1 Corinthians 13:4-7 *Love is patient and kind. Love is not jealous or boastful or proud or rude. Love does not demand its own way. Love is not irritable, and it keeps no record of when it has been wronged. It is never glad about injustice but rejoices whenever the truth wins out. Love never gives up, never loses faith, is always hopeful, and endures through every circumstance.*

We can show affection for our spouses in the way we respond to them.

Ephesians 5:25 *And you husbands must love your wives with the same love Christ showed the church. He gave up his life for her.*
Total devotion and dedication mirror affection. Love and affection are not for the moment but forever. Christ loved the church enough to die for it. Commit that your love for your spouse will be as strong.

Song of Songs 1:7-8 *"Tell me, O my love, where are you leading your flock today? Where will you rest your sheep at noon? For why should I wander like a prostitute among the flocks of your companions?" Young Man: "If you don't know, O most beautiful woman, follow the trail of my flock to the shepherds' tents, and there feed your young goats."*
Wanting to spend time with one another communicates our level of affection for each other.

Song of Songs 2:4 *He brings me to the banquet hall, so everyone can see how much he loves me.*
We can let others know our delight with our spouses.

Song of Songs 1:12 *Young Woman: "The king is lying on his couch, enchanted by the fragrance of my perfume."*
We can look for ways to please one another—for instance, wearing his or her favorite perfume or cologne.

18

Where should we focus our affections?

Mark 12:30 *And you must love the Lord your God with all your heart, all your soul, all your mind, and all your strength.*

Psalm 42:1-2 *As the deer pants for streams of water, so I long for you, O God. I thirst for God, the living God. When can I come and stand before him?*

Psalm 73:25 *Whom have I in heaven but you? I desire you more than anything on earth.*
Our primary affection should be for God.

How should we respond if we feel our affections are waning or misplaced?

Revelation 2:4-5 *But I have this complaint against you. You don't love me or each other as you did at first! Look how far you have fallen from your first love! Turn back to me again and work as you did at first.*
We should be aware of our indifference and turn back to God. If our indifference is to our spouse, we should work to rekindle the fire together.

Psalm 106:12-13 *Then at last his people believed his promises. Then they finally sang his praise. Yet how quickly they forgot what he had done! They wouldn't wait for his counsel!*
We should remember what God has done for us in the past and wait for his counsel today. We should also remember the times of passion and

19

affection with our spouses and reflect on those together.

Proverbs 4:23 *Above all else, guard your heart, for it affects everything you do.*
We should be careful to guard our affections, realizing their effect on our lives—for good or bad.

PROMISE FROM GOD: 1 Peter 4:8 *Most important of all, continue to show deep love for each other, for love covers a multitude of sins.*

Age/Aging

How should age affect our marriage commitment?

Proverbs 5:18-19 *Let your wife be a fountain of blessing for you. Rejoice in the wife of your youth. She is a loving doe, a graceful deer. . . . May you always be captivated by her love.*

Malachi 2:15-16 *Didn't the LORD make you one with your wife? In body and spirit you are his. And what does he want? Godly children from your union. So guard yourself; remain loyal to the wife of your youth. "For I hate divorce!" says the LORD, the God of Israel. . . . "So guard yourself; always remain loyal to your wife."*

We are to enjoy our spouses throughout our lives. We are to remain loyal to one another as long as we live, "'til death do us part."

What can lead to a longer life?

Psalm 128:1,6 *How happy are those who fear the LORD—all who follow his ways! . . . May you live to enjoy your grandchildren.*

Proverbs 3:1-2 *My child, never forget the things I have taught you. Store my commands in your heart, for they will give you a long and satisfying life.*
Fear of the Lord, which involves knowing and obeying the Lord and his commands, always leads to a satisfying life and often leads to a long life as well. God's word shows us how to avoid those things that are bad for us. Is it surprising that a close relationship with the Author of Life enriches and lengthens our lives?

Ephesians 6:2-3 *"Honor your father and mother." This is the first of the Ten Commandments that ends with a promise. And this is the promise: If you honor your father and mother, you will live a long life, full of blessing.*
God promises that those who treat their father and mother with respect will live a long life.

Psalm 34:11-14 *Come, my children, and listen to me, and I will teach you to fear the LORD. Do any of you want to live a life that is long and good? Then*

21

watch your tongue! Keep your lips from telling lies!
Turn away from evil and do good. Work hard at
living in peace with others.
Shunning evil and embracing good lead to a
long, good life because we avoid those things that
harm and endanger us. Wickedness brings a
spiritual cancer that eats away at our souls.

Proverbs 3:13,16 *Happy is the person who*
finds wisdom and gains understanding. . . .
[Wisdom] offers you life in her right hand, and riches
and honor in her left.
Living with wisdom and understanding can lead
to a long and honorable life. Wisdom and
understanding bring mental, social, and spiritual
transformation.

PROMISE FROM GOD: Isaiah 46:4 *I*
will be your God throughout your lifetime—until your
hair is white with age. I made you, and I will care for
you. I will carry you along and save you.

Aggravate

How can we avoid aggravating one another?

Proverbs 25:20 *Singing cheerful songs to a person*
whose heart is heavy is as bad as stealing someone's
jacket in cold weather or rubbing salt in a wound.

Ignoring others' pain or responding to their pain inappropriately can aggravate them.

Proverbs 15:1 *A gentle answer turns away wrath, but harsh words stir up anger.*
Harsh words can aggravate others.

Proverbs 25:23 *As surely as a wind from the north brings rain, so a gossiping tongue causes anger!*
Gossip can spread angry, judgmental attitudes—aggravating bad feelings between people.

How should we respond to being aggravated?

Psalm 4:4 *Don't sin by letting anger gain control over you. Think about it overnight and remain silent.*

James 1:19 *Dear friends, be quick to listen, slow to speak, and slow to get angry.*
Remain under God's control. Slow down and carefully think through how you will respond to those who annoy you.

Proverbs 14:29 *Those who control their anger have great understanding; those with a hasty temper will make mistakes.*

Ephesians 4:26-27 *Don't sin by letting anger gain control over you. Don't let the sun go down while you are still angry, for anger gives a mighty foothold to the Devil.*

Avoid any reaction based on anger. Anger is like a forest fire—it quickly destroys that which takes a long time to replace.

What can be particularly aggravating in a marriage relationship?

Proverbs 25:24 *It is better to live alone in the corner of an attic than with a contentious wife in a lovely home.*
A quarrelsome or nagging spouse is annoying. We should each assess ourselves!

PROMISE FROM GOD: Psalm 145:8 *The LORD is kind and merciful, slow to get angry, full of unfailing love.*

Anger

What are the effects of anger?

Genesis 27:41-43 *Esau hated Jacob because he had stolen his blessing, and he said to himself. . . . "I will kill Jacob." But someone got wind of what Esau was planning and reported it to Rebekah. She sent for Jacob and told him . . . "Flee to your uncle Laban in Haran."*
Anger isolates us from others.

Psalm 37:8 *Stop your anger! . . . Do not envy others—it only leads to harm.*

James 1:20 *Your anger can never make things right in God's sight.*
Anger can produce ungodliness and evil motives in us.

1 Samuel 20:30-31 *Saul boiled with rage at Jonathan. . . . "As long as that son of Jesse is alive, you'll never be king. Now go and get him so I can kill him!"*
Anger can blind us to what is good and right. Saul's jealous anger blinded him to the fact that David was God's choice to be the next king.

Genesis 4:4-5, 8 *The LORD accepted Abel and his offering, but he did not accept Cain and his offering. This made Cain very angry. . . . Later. . . . Cain attacked and killed his brother.*
Anger can lead to violence—even murder.

How should I deal with my own anger in relationships?

Ephesians 4:26 *Don't sin by letting anger gain control over you. Don't let the sun go down while you are still angry.*

Ephesians 4:31-32 *Get rid of all bitterness, rage, anger, harsh words, and slander, as well as all types of malicious behavior. Instead, be kind to each other, tenderhearted, forgiving one another, just as God through Christ has forgiven you.*

Proverbs 19:11 *People with good sense restrain their anger; they earn esteem by overlooking wrongs.*
Anger must be dealt with quickly before it becomes bitterness, hatred, or revenge. Kindness and forgiveness melt anger away.

What is the best way to deal with an angry person?

Proverbs 29:8 *Mockers can get a whole town agitated, but those who are wise will calm anger.*

Proverbs 15:1 *A gentle answer turns away wrath, but harsh words stir up anger.*

Proverbs 22:24-25 *Keep away from angry, short-tempered people, or you will learn to be like them and endanger your soul.*
Reacting to anger with anger almost always intensifies the problem. Wisdom and gentleness almost always calm an angry person.

PROMISE FROM GOD: Psalm 103:8 *The Lord is merciful and gracious; he is slow to get angry and full of unfailing love.*

Apologize

To whom should we apologize?

Psalm 51:4 *Against you, and you alone, have I sinned; I have done what is evil in your sight.*

1 Chronicles 21:8 *Then David said to God, "I have sinned greatly and shouldn't have taken the census. Please forgive me for doing this foolish thing."*

Luke 15:18 *I will go home to my father and say, "Father, I have sinned against both heaven and you."*

Matthew 18:15 *If another believer sins against you, go privately and point out the fault. If the other person listens and confesses it, you have won that person back.*

While our sins should always be confessed to God, we should also apologize to those affected by our wrong. An apology may not remove the wrong we have done, but it may make room for forgiveness, remove some of the pain, and bring about a restoration of the relationship.

How do we apologize?

Numbers 14:19-20 *"Please pardon the sins of this people because of your magnificent, unfailing love, just as you have forgiven them ever since they left Egypt." Then the LORD said, "I will pardon them as you have requested."*

"I'm sorry" is a great start. Then ask forgiveness based on God's unfailing love and his promise to supply it.

Luke 15:21 *His son said to him, "Father, I have sinned against both heaven and you, and I am no longer worthy of being called your son."*

27

We should apologize honestly and humbly.
Don't try to justify what you did or blame others
for it. Confess your wrongs and ask forgiveness.

1 Samuel 12:3 *"Now tell me as I stand before the
LORD and before his anointed one—whose ox or donkey
have I stolen? Have I ever cheated any of you? Have I
ever oppressed you? Have I ever taken a bribe? Tell me
and I will make right whatever I have done wrong."*
An apology may include restitution. What can
you do to compensate for your wrong?

Jeremiah 3:10 *"But in spite of all this, her
faithless sister Judah has never sincerely returned to me.
She has only pretended to be sorry," says the LORD.*
The sincerity of an apology is measured by
changed behavior. Apologetic hands and feet
must follow apologetic lips.

How do we accept an apology?

Psalm 51:17 *The sacrifice you want is a broken
spirit. A broken and repentant heart, O God, you will
not despise.*

2 Samuel 12:13 *Then David confessed to
Nathan, "I have sinned against the LORD." Nathan
replied, "Yes, but the LORD has forgiven you, and you
won't die for this sin."*
The Lord welcomes a broken and repentant heart.
That's a good model to follow when others
apologize to us.

1 Samuel 25:35 *Then David accepted her gifts and told her, "Return home in peace. We will not kill your husband."*

Luke 17:3 *I am warning you! If another believer sins, rebuke him; then if he repents, forgive him.* We, too, are to be forgiving. True forgiveness is not grudging or sparing but generous and joyful.

PROMISE FROM GOD: Proverbs 28:13-14 *People who cover over their sins will not prosper. But if they confess and forsake them, they will receive mercy. Blessed are those who have a tender conscience, but the stubborn are headed for serious trouble.*

Appreciation

Whom should we appreciate?

Ephesians 5:22-24 *You wives will submit to your husbands as you do to the Lord. For a husband is the head of his wife as Christ is the head of his body, the church; he gave his life to be her Savior. As the church submits to Christ, so you wives must submit to your husbands in everything.*

1 Peter 3:1 *In the same way, you wives must accept the authority of your husbands, even those who refuse to accept the Good News. Your godly lives will speak to them better than any words.*

1 Corinthians 7:14 *For the Christian wife brings holiness to her marriage, and the Christian husband brings holiness to his marriage. Otherwise, your children would not have a godly influence, but now they are set apart for him.*

A wife is to appreciate her husband's authority over her and love for her. She is to value what her husband adds to the home.

Proverbs 18:22 *The man who finds a wife finds a treasure and receives favor from the LORD.*

Proverbs 19:14 *Parents can provide their sons with an inheritance of houses and wealth, but only the LORD can give an understanding wife.*

Proverbs 31:10 *Who can find a virtuous and capable wife? She is worth more than precious rubies.*

Ephesians 5:25, 28 *You husbands must love your wives with the same love Christ showed the church. He gave up his life for her. . . . In the same way, husbands ought to love their wives as they love their own bodies. For a man is actually loving himself when he loves his wife.*

A husband should appreciate his wife as a treasure from the Lord. Husbands, how would you respond if someone gave you a million dollars? Now go and respond that way to your wife—she is a far greater gift!

How can we let others know we appreciate them?

Colossians 3:18 *You wives must submit to your husbands, as is fitting for those who belong to the Lord.*
A wife can show appreciation for her husband by submitting to him.

Proverbs 31:28-29 *Her children stand and bless her. Her husband praises her: "There are many virtuous and capable women in the world, but you surpass them all!"*

1 Peter 3:7 *In the same way, you husbands must give honor to your wives. Treat her with understanding as you live together. She may be weaker than you are, but she is your equal partner in God's gift of new life. If you don't treat her as you should, your prayers will not be heard.*
A husband can show his appreciation by honoring his wife both privately and publicly. Children can show their appreciation by saying thank you.

Ephesians 1:16-17 *I have never stopped thanking God for you. I pray for you constantly, asking God, the glorious Father of our Lord Jesus Christ, to give you spiritual wisdom and understanding, so that you might grow in your knowledge of God.*
Thank God for those you appreciate, and tell them about it!

Luke 17:15-16 *One of them, when he saw that he was healed, came back to Jesus, shouting, "Praise God, I'm healed!" He fell face down on the ground at Jesus' feet, thanking him for what he had done.* The simplest form of showing appreciation, saying "thank you," is often overlooked. Find a way to say "thank you" every day to someone you love.

Luke 7:36-38 *One of the Pharisees asked Jesus to come to his home for a meal, so Jesus accepted the invitation and sat down to eat. A certain immoral woman heard he was there and brought a beautiful jar filled with expensive perfume. Then she knelt behind him at his feet, weeping. Her tears fell on his feet, and she wiped them off with her hair. Then she kept kissing his feet and putting perfume on them.* Our actions show our appreciation.

How do we become appreciative?

Psalm 35:28 *Then I will tell everyone of your justice and goodness, and I will praise you all day long.*

Philippians 1:3-4 *Every time I think of you, I give thanks to my God. I always pray for you, and I make my requests with a heart full of joy.*

1 Thessalonians 5:18 *No matter what happens, always be thankful, for this is God's will for you who belong to Christ Jesus.*

1 Chronicles 23:30 *And each morning and evening they stood before the LORD to sing songs of thanks and praise to him.*
Cultivate an appreciative heart by giving thanks regularly, consistently, and spontaneously.

PROMISE FROM GOD: Psalm 92:1-2 *It is good to give thanks to the LORD, to sing praises to the Most High. It is good to proclaim your unfailing love in the morning, your faithfulness in the evening.*

Attention

How can we pay more attention to God?

Ezekiel 40:4 *He said to me, "Son of man, watch and listen. Pay close attention to everything I show you. You have been brought here so I can show you many things."*
When God is a regular part of our thoughts, we are more prone to notice what he is doing.

1 Kings 19:11-13 *And after the earthquake there was a fire, but the LORD was not in the fire. And after the fire there was the sound of a gentle whisper. When Elijah heard it, he wrapped his face in his cloak and went out and stood at the entrance of the cave. And a voice said, "What are you doing here, Elijah?"*

Psalm 46:10 *Be silent, and know that I am God! I will be honored by every nation. I will be honored throughout the world.*
A still, quiet spirit helps us to give our attention to God.

Hebrews 3:15 *But never forget the warning: "Today you must listen to his voice. Don't harden your hearts against him as Israel did when they rebelled."*

Proverbs 4:20 *Pay attention, my child, to what I say. Listen carefully.*
We should make listening to God an immediate priority.

Psalm 78:1 *O my people, listen to my teaching. Open your ears to what I am saying.*

Matthew 13:9, 12 *Anyone who is willing to hear should listen and understand! . . . To those who are open to my teaching, more understanding will be given.*
A willing attitude helps us pay attention to God. Listening is not merely an action, it's also an attitude. As your respect for someone withers, so will your listening. As your love for someone grows, so will your listening.

Ezekiel 12:2 *Son of man, you live among rebels who could see the truth if they wanted to, but they don't want to. They could hear me if they would listen, but they won't listen because they are rebellious.*

Jeremiah 17:23 *They did not listen or obey.*
They stubbornly refused to pay attention and would
not respond to discipline.
A rebellious or proud spirit can keep us from
paying attention to God. Rebellion and pride
turn our affections inward. Humility turns our
affections outward.

How can we pay better attention to our loved one?

Song of Songs 8:13 *O my beloved, lingering*
in the gardens, how wonderful that your companions
can listen to your voice. Let me hear it, too!
It's difficult to pay attention to someone if he or
she isn't nearby. Proximity should enhance our
ability and desire to pay attention to one another.

Hebrews 5:11 *There is so much more we would*
like to say about this. But you don't seem to listen, so
it's hard to make you understand.
We should try to understand what others are
saying. Hearing words and listening to their
meaning are two different things.

Proverbs 12:15 *Fools think they need no advice,*
but the wise listen to others.

Proverbs 15:31-32 *If you listen to constructive*
criticism, you will be at home among the wise. If you
reject criticism, you only harm yourself; but if you
listen to correction, you grow in understanding.

Realizing the benefit of advice and constructive criticism helps us to be more attentive to what others have to say. Listening may change our lives.

PROMISES FROM GOD: Psalm 116:2 *Because he bends down and listens, I will pray as long as I have breath!*

1 Timothy 4:16 *Keep a close watch on yourself and on your teaching. Stay true to what is right, and God will save you and those who hear you.*

Available

How does God make himself available to us?

Psalm 139:8-10 *If I go up to heaven, you are there; if I go down to the place of the dead, you are there. If I ride the wings of the morning, if I dwell by the farthest oceans, even there your hand will guide me, and your strength will support me.*

Matthew 28:20 *"Be sure of this: I am with you always, even to the end of the age."*

Isaiah 43:2 *When you go through deep waters and great trouble, I will be with you.*

Psalm 46:1 *God is our refuge and strength, always ready to help in times of trouble.*

God's presence and help are available to us every moment and everywhere. He is always with us, ready to listen and to surround us with his love.

Colossians 1:27 *For it has pleased God to tell his people that the riches and glory of Christ are for you Gentiles, too. For this is the secret: Christ lives in you, and this is your assurance that you will share in his glory.*

God is available to us through his Son, Jesus Christ. When we become God's children, Christ actually lives in us!

To whom should we make ourselves available?

Romans 12:13 *When God's children are in need, be the one to help them out. And get into the habit of inviting guests home for dinner or, if they need lodging, for the night.*

Exodus 23:5 *If you see the donkey of someone who hates you struggling beneath a heavy load, do not walk by. Instead, stop and offer to help.*

Matthew 25:34-36, 40 *"Come, you who are blessed by my Father, inherit the Kingdom prepared for you from the foundation of the world. For I was hungry, and you fed me. I was thirsty, and you gave me a drink. I was a stranger, and you invited me into your home. I was naked, and you gave me clothing. I was sick, and you cared for me. I was in prison, and*

you visited me. . . . I assure you, when you did it to one of the least of these my brothers and sisters, you were doing it to me!"
We should be available to those in need—family members, fellow Christians, friends, and enemies. Available hands reflect an available heart.

PROMISE FROM GOD: Isaiah 41:13 *I am holding you by your right hand—I, the LORD your God. And I say to you, "Do not be afraid. I am here to help you."*

Avoidance/Avoiding

What should we avoid?

1 Thessalonians 5:22 *Keep away from every kind of evil.*
Avoid every evil.

1 John 5:21 *Dear children, keep away from anything that might take God's place in your hearts.*

1 Corinthians 10:14 *So, my dear friends, flee from the worship of idols.*
Avoid worshiping anything or anyone but God alone.

Proverbs 4:24 *Avoid all perverse talk; stay far from corrupt speech.*

Philippians 2:14 *In everything you do, stay away from complaining and arguing.*

2 Timothy 2:23 *Again I say, don't get involved in foolish, ignorant arguments that only start fights.*

Proverbs 20:3 *Avoiding a fight is a mark of honor; only fools insist on quarreling.*
Avoid unholy talk.

How do we avoid the things we should?

Job 1:8 *Then the LORD asked Satan, "Have you noticed my servant Job? He is the finest man in all the earth—a man of complete integrity. He fears God and will have nothing to do with evil."*

Romans 13:14 *But let the Lord Jesus Christ take control of you, and don't think of ways to indulge your evil desires.*
Keeping a close relationship with the Lord God helps us to avoid evil. The closer we are to God, the farther we are from evil.

Colossians 3:5 *So put to death the sinful, earthly things lurking within you. Have nothing to do with sexual sin, impurity, lust, and shameful desires. Don't be greedy for the good things of this life, for that is idolatry.*
Turn your back on evil and your face toward God.

Proverbs 3:6-7 *Seek his will in all you do, and he will direct your paths. Don't be impressed with*

*your own wisdom. Instead, fear the LORD and turn
your back on evil.*
Keep your confidence in the Lord's wisdom and
not in yourself. Seek his will and not your own.

PROMISE FROM GOD: Proverbs 16:17
*The path of the upright leads away from evil; whoever
follows that path is safe.*

Balance

How did Jesus live a balanced life?

John 5:19 *Jesus replied, "I assure you, the Son can
do nothing by himself. He does only what he sees the
Father doing. Whatever the Father does, the Son also
does."*
Jesus walked in the Father's footsteps.

Luke 2:52 *So Jesus grew both in height and in
wisdom, and he was loved by God and by all who
knew him.*
Jesus grew in all areas: physically, mentally,
spiritually, and emotionally.

John 2:1-2 *The next day Jesus' mother was a
guest at a wedding celebration in the village of Cana
in Galilee. Jesus and his disciples were also invited to
the celebration.*

Mark 6:31-32 *Then Jesus said, "Let's get away from the crowds for a while and rest." There were so many people coming and going that Jesus and his apostles didn't even have time to eat. They left by boat for a quieter spot.*
Jesus saw the importance of spending time with people and the importance of rest and quiet. Life is both work and play, seriousness and fun.

How do we find the proper balance in life?

James 3:13 *If you are wise and understand God's ways, live a life of steady goodness so that only good deeds will pour forth. And if you don't brag about the good you do, then you will be truly wise!*
A godly life is a balanced life. If we actively look to God, he will help us keep balance in our lives.

Proverbs 12:3 *Wickedness never brings stability; only the godly have deep roots.*
A balanced life is one in step with God. Finding and maintaining the proper balance in life depend on the depth of our relationship with God.

Romans 12:2 *Don't copy the behavior and customs of this world, but let God transform you into a new person by changing the way you think. Then you will know what God wants you to do, and you will know how good and pleasing and perfect his will really is.*

When we let God change our thinking to reflect his thinking, he will show us what to do and how to live by his priorities and his will.

1 Peter 1:13 *So think clearly and exercise self-control. Look forward to the special blessings that will come to you at the return of Jesus Christ.*
A life of self-control is a balanced life.

Romans 12:4-5 *Just as our bodies have many parts and each part has a special function, so it is with Christ's body. We are all parts of his one body, and each of us has different work to do.*

2 Timothy 1:6 *This is why I remind you to fan into flames the spiritual gift God gave you when I laid my hands on you.*
A balanced life makes full use of God's gifts.

Titus 2:12 *And we are instructed to turn from godless living and sinful pleasures. We should live in this evil world with self-control, right conduct, and devotion to God.*
A balanced life avoids compromise with ungodliness. Ungodliness causes us to lose control.

Psalm 139:3 *You chart the path ahead of me and tell me where to stop and rest. Every moment you know where I am.*
Trusting God to chart the steps of our lives will help us live a balanced life. God will give us what we need.

What causes our lives to become unbalanced?

James 3:16 *Wherever there is jealousy and selfish ambition, there you will find disorder and every kind of evil.*
Our lives become unbalanced when we dwell on earthly things instead of depending on God's wisdom.

Hebrews 13:5 *Stay away from the love of money; be satisfied with what you have. For God has said, "I will never fail you. I will never forsake you."*
Feelings of dissatisfaction often result in an unbalanced life. Focusing selfishly on acquiring things inhibits our loving and serving God. The godly find contentment in him.

Proverbs 23:21 *Too much sleep clothes a person with rags.*

2 Corinthians 8:12-13 *God wants you to give what you have, not what you don't have. Of course, I don't mean you should give so much that you suffer from having too little.*
Excess often leads to imbalance. Too much of anything means there is not enough of something else.

Proverbs 10:21 *The godly give good advice, but fools are destroyed by their lack of common sense.*
Common sense can help us lead balanced lives.

PROMISE FROM GOD: James 1:25 *If you keep looking steadily into God's perfect law—the law that sets you free—and if you do what it says and don't forget what you heard, then God will bless you for doing it.*

Betrayal

How can we avoid betraying others?

Proverbs 11:13 *A gossip goes around revealing secrets, but those who are trustworthy can keep a confidence.*
Avoid gossiping and gossipers.

Proverbs 25:18 *Telling lies about others is as harmful as hitting them with an ax, wounding them with a sword, or shooting them with a sharp arrow.*
Tell the truth and never speak lies about another.

Psalm 55:20 *As for this friend of mine, he betrayed me; he broke his promises.*
Keep your promises.

Proverbs 19:22 *Loyalty makes a person attractive. And it is better to be poor than dishonest.*

Proverbs 3:3 *Never let loyalty and kindness get away from you! Wear them like a necklace; write them deep within your heart.*
Practice loyalty and kindness to others.

Malachi 2:14-16 *You cry out, "Why has the LORD abandoned us?" I'll tell you why! Because the LORD witnessed the vows you and your wife made to each other on your wedding day when you were young. But you have been disloyal to her, though she remained your faithful companion, the wife of your marriage vows. . . . So guard yourself; always remain loyal to your wife."*

Unfaithfulness and disloyalty in a marriage is betrayal. Always be faithful and loyal to your spouse.

What should we do when we feel betrayed?

Matthew 10:21 *Brother will betray brother to death, fathers will betray their own children, and children will rise against their parents and cause them to be killed.*

Betrayal is a part of everyone's experience—even Christians'. Expect it and you will be more prepared for it.

Luke 22:33-34 *Peter said, "Lord, I am ready to go to prison with you, and even to die with you." But Jesus said, "Peter, let me tell you something. The rooster will not crow tomorrow morning until you have denied three times that you even know me."*

Love those who betray you, as Jesus did (Luke 22:32; John 21:15-19). Love the betrayer, but not the act of betrayal.

45

Ephesians 4:31-32 *Get rid of all bitterness, rage, anger, harsh words, and slander, as well as all types of malicious behavior. Instead, be kind to each other, tenderhearted, forgiving one another, just as God through Christ has forgiven you.*

Genesis 50:19-20 *But Joseph told them, "Don't be afraid of me. Am I God, to judge and punish you? As far as I am concerned, God turned into good what you meant for evil. He brought me to the high position I have today so I could save the lives of many people."* We are to forgive even someone who betrays us.

PROMISE FROM GOD: Isaiah 54:10 *"For the mountains may depart and the hills disappear, but even then I will remain loyal to you. My covenant of blessing will never be broken," says the LORD, who has mercy on you.*

Bother

see Aggravate

Boundaries

What are God's boundaries for us?

Micah 6:8 *No, O people, the LORD has already told you what is good, and this is what he requires: to do what is right, to love mercy, and to walk humbly with your God.*

God's boundaries for us are that we do what is right, show mercy to others, and pursue a proper relationship with him.

Deuteronomy 10:12-13 *And now, Israel, what does the LORD your God require of you? He requires you to fear him, to live according to his will, to love and worship him with all your heart and soul, and to obey the LORD's commands and laws that I am giving you today for your own good.*
Reverence for God should mark out the boundaries of our lives. These boundaries include living in accord with God's will, worshiping him wholeheartedly, and obeying all his commands.

Ecclesiastes 3:1 *There is a time for everything, a season for every activity under heaven.*
God provides the boundaries of seasons and time.

How do we set boundaries for ourselves?

Romans 12:2 *Don't copy the behavior and customs of this world, but let God transform you into a new person by changing the way you think. Then you will know what God wants you to do, and you will know how good and pleasing and perfect his will really is.*
Study God's word to find out how to live and how to be transformed by his power and presence. His word provides the proper boundaries for living.

1 Corinthians 7:35 *I am saying this for your benefit, not to place restrictions on you. I want you to do whatever will help you serve the Lord best, with as few distractions as possible.*
Serving the Lord is a lifetime priority. It guides us in setting boundaries. Rather than restricting us, it gets rid of distractions that can keep us from accomplishing magnificent things.

1 Corinthians 10:29, 33 *It might not be a matter of conscience for you, but it is for the other person. . . . I try to please everyone in everything I do. I don't just do what I like or what is best for me, but what is best for them so they may be saved.*
We should consider others when setting our personal boundaries. Part of the reason we set up personal boundaries is to keep us from hurting others and causing them to stumble.

PROMISE FROM GOD: Deuteronomy 10:12-13 *And now, Israel, what does the LORD your God require of you? He requires you to fear him, to live according to his will, to love and worship him with all your heart and soul, and to obey the LORD's commands and laws that I am giving you today for your own good.*

Challenges

How are we to face life's greatest challenges?

2 Samuel 22:30 *In your strength I can crush an army; with my God I can scale any wall.*

Psalm 37:5 *Commit everything you do to the LORD. Trust him, and he will help you.*

Ephesians 3:20 *Now glory be to God! By his mighty power at work within us, he is able to accomplish infinitely more than we would ever dare to ask or hope.*

Regardless of the size of the task, God's strength working in us is sufficient to help us see the job through to completion. There is no job too big for God.

How can we challenge one another?

Isaiah 41:6 *They encourage one another with the words, "Be strong!"*

Ephesians 6:10 *A final word: Be strong with the Lord's mighty power.*

We are to encourage one another to be strong in our obedience to God and to hold on to his promises and power.

Luke 17:3 *I am warning you! If another believer sins, rebuke him; then if he repents, forgive him.*

We are to challenge one another to live righteously.

1 Thessalonians 5:14 *Brothers and sisters, we urge you to warn those who are lazy. Encourage those who are timid. Take tender care of those who are weak. Be patient with everyone.*

2 Timothy 4:2 *Preach the word of God. Be persistent, whether the time is favorable or not. Patiently correct, rebuke, and encourage your people with good teaching.*
God calls us to speak to others in ways that will help them grow.

PROMISE FROM GOD: Ephesians 6:10 *A final word: Be strong with the Lord's mighty power. Put on all of God's armor so that you will be able to stand firm against all strategies and tricks of the Devil.*

Change

With all the change in our lives, what can help us keep it all together?

Lamentations 5:19 *But LORD, you remain the same forever! Your throne continues from generation to generation.*

James 1:17 *God above, who created all heaven's lights . . . never changes or casts shifting shadows.*

Hebrews 1:12 *You are always the same.*

Psalm 59:10 *In his unfailing love, my God will come and help me.*
We can trust the character of God—he is unchanging and completely reliable.

Hebrews 13:8 *Jesus Christ is the same yesterday, today, and forever.*
We can place our faith in Jesus Christ, whose love and grace are eternal.

Mark 13:31 *Heaven and earth will disappear, but my words will remain forever.*
We can build our lives on God's word because its truth will never change.

Genesis 37:28 *When the traders came by, his brothers pulled Joseph out of the pit and sold him for twenty pieces of silver.*

Romans 8:28 *We know that God causes everything to work together for the good of those who love God and are called according to his purpose for them.*
God can work his will even through traumatic, unpredictable, and unfair change.

Matthew 1:18-25 *An angel of the Lord appeared to him in a dream. . . . When Joseph woke up, he did what the angel of the Lord commanded.*
When our neatly laid plans are changed, we can still find peace in obeying the call of God.

How do we change the areas in our lives needing to be changed?

Acts 3:19 *Now turn from your sins and turn to God, so you can be cleansed of your sins.*
If you haven't repented of your sins, this is the area of life in greatest need of change.

Psalm 51:10 *Create in me a clean heart, O God. Renew a right spirit within me.*

Romans 12:2 *Don't copy the behavior and customs of this world, but let God transform you into a new person by changing the way you think. Then you will know what God wants you to do, and you will know how good and pleasing and perfect his will really is.*

Ephesians 4:23-24 *There must be a spiritual renewal of your thoughts and attitudes. You must display a new nature because you are a new person, created in God's likeness—righteous, holy, and true.*
Real change occurs when we ask God for a new heart filled with Christ's love. He will give us a new spirit to show us how to live, a new way of thinking, and a new attitude.

How do we promote positive change in others?

2 Timothy 2:23-25 *Don't get involved in foolish, ignorant arguments that only start fights. The Lord's servants must not quarrel but must be kind to everyone. . . . They should gently teach those who*

oppose the truth. Perhaps God will change those people's hearts, and they will believe the truth. We will accomplish more when we don't try to change others but point them to God so that he can do the changing.

PROMISES FROM GOD: Isaiah 40:8 *The grass withers, and the flowers fade, but the word of our God stands forever.*

2 Corinthians 5:17 *Those who become Christians become new persons. They are not the same anymore, for the old life is gone. A new life has begun!*

Chaos

see **Confusion**

Childlessness

see **Infertility**

Children

What is the relationship God intended between parents and their children?

Ephesians 6:1-4 *Children, obey your parents because you belong to the Lord, for this is the right* thing to do. "Honor your father and mother." This is the first of the Ten Commandments that ends with a promise. And this is the promise: If you honor your father and mother, "you will live a long life, full of blessing." And now a word to you fathers. Don't make your children angry by the way you treat them. Rather, bring them up with the discipline and instruction approved by the Lord.

Parents are to discipline in love and to teach their children to walk in God's ways. Children are to respond with respect and obedience.

How can we most effectively teach our children about God and His ways?

Deuteronomy 11:18-19 So commit yourselves completely to these words of mine. Tie them to your hands as a reminder, and wear them on your forehead. Teach them to your children. Talk about them when you are at home and when you are away on a journey, when you are lying down and when you are getting up again.

Proverbs 22:6 Teach your children to choose the right path, and when they are older, they will remain upon it.

Exodus 10:2 You will be able to tell wonderful stories to your children and grandchildren about the marvelous things I am doing among the Egyptians to prove that I am the LORD.

The best way to teach our children God's ways is to continually live them out ourselves.

PROMISE FROM GOD: Isaiah 59:21
My Spirit will not leave them, and neither will these words I have given you. They will be on your lips and on the lips of your children and your children's children forever.

Choices

see **Decisions**

Church

What is the purpose of the church?

Acts 2:47 *And each day the Lord added to their group those who were being saved.*
The church is a community of individuals and families who are saved by faith in Christ.

1 Corinthians 3:16-17 *Don't you realize that all of you together are the temple of God and that the Spirit of God lives in you? God will bring ruin upon anyone who ruins this temple. For God's temple is holy, and you Christians are that temple.*
The church is God's dwelling place. It should exhibit God's holiness to its members and to the world.

1 Corinthians 12:12-13 *The human body has many parts, but the many parts make up only one body. So it is with the body of Christ. Some of us are Jews, some are Gentiles, some are slaves, and some are free. But we have all been baptized into Christ's body by one Spirit, and we have all received the same Spirit.* The church should exhibit the unity and reconciliation made possible solely through Christ by his Spirit.

Revelation 19:7-8 *Let us be glad and rejoice and honor him. For the time has come for the wedding feast of the Lamb, and his bride has prepared herself. She is permitted to wear the finest white linen.* The church is Christ's bride, created for intimate fellowship with the Lord.

Why should we be involved in church?

Psalm 27:4 *The one thing I ask of the LORD—the thing I seek most—is to live in the house of the LORD all the days of my life, delighting in the LORD's perfections and meditating in his Temple.*

Psalm 84:4 *How happy are those who can live in your house, always singing your praises.* Even though God lives in the heart of every believer, he also lives in the community of the church. When the church is gathered together, it meets with God in a special way.

Ephesians 2:19-21 *You are citizens along with all of God's holy people. You are members of God's family. We are his house, built on the foundation of the apostles and the prophets. And the cornerstone is Christ Jesus himself. We who believe are carefully joined together, becoming a holy temple for the Lord.*
All believers are joined together in God's family. By meeting together we can experience this reality.

Hebrews 10:25 *Let us not neglect our meeting together, as some people do, but encourage and warn each other, especially now that the day of his coming back again is drawing near.*
When we meet together, we should build each other up and help each other. By definition, fellowship involves joining together with other believers!

PROMISE FROM GOD: Matthew 16:18 *I will build my church, and all the powers of hell will not conquer it.*

Comfort

How can we comfort others?

Job 42:11 *Then all his brothers, sisters, and former friends came and feasted with him in his home. And they consoled him and comforted him because of all the trials the LORD had brought against him.*

We can comfort others by being with them.

Job 21:2 *Listen closely to what I am saying. You can console me by listening to me.*
We can comfort others by listening to what they say.

Ruth 2:13 *"I hope I continue to please you, sir," she replied. "You have comforted me by speaking so kindly to me, even though I am not as worthy as your workers."*

1 Corinthians 14:3 *But one who prophesies is helping others grow in the Lord, encouraging and comforting them.*
We can speak kind and encouraging words to others.

Philemon 1:7 *I myself have gained much joy and comfort from your love, my brother, because your kindness has so often refreshed the hearts of God's people.*
Love expressed through kind actions can comfort and encourage others.

PROMISES FROM GOD: Psalm 147:3 *He heals the brokenhearted, binding up their wounds.*

2 Corinthians 1:5 *The more we suffer for Christ, the more God will shower us with his comfort through Christ.*

Commitment

What is involved in being committed to God?

Psalm 37:5 *Commit everything you do to the LORD. Trust him, and he will help you.*

Proverbs 3:6 *Seek [God's] will in all you do, and he will direct your paths.*
Commitment to the Lord manifests itself in obedient trust.

Exodus 24:3 *The people . . . answered in unison, "We will do everything the LORD has told us to do."*

John 17:4 *"I brought glory to you here on earth by doing everything you told me to do."*
Commitment to the Lord involves doing everything he has told us to do.

Daniel 3:17-18 *If we are thrown into the blazing furnace, the God whom we serve is able to save us. . . . But even if he doesn't, Your Majesty can be sure that we will never serve your gods.*
Commitment is being willing to suffer the consequences of obedience.

Romans 6:13 *Give yourselves completely to God since you have been given new life. And use your whole body as a tool to do what is right for the glory of God.*
Wholehearted commitment to God involves giving him everything—even our bodies—to use as he wishes.

Amos 5:24 *I want to see a mighty flood of justice, a river of righteous living that will never run dry.*
Commitment to God means commitment to do good to other people.

Why is commitment important?

Psalm 25:10 *The LORD leads with unfailing love and faithfulness all those who keep his covenant and obey his decrees.*
God lovingly and faithfully leads his committed followers.

Psalm 31:23 *For the LORD protects those who are loyal to him.*
God watches over those who are loyal to him.

Ruth 1:16 *I will go wherever you go and live wherever you live. Your people will be my people, and your God will be my God.*
Commitment is a mark of true friendship.

1 Corinthians 13:7 *Love never gives up, never loses faith, is always hopeful, and endures through every circumstance.*
Loyal commitment is love in action.

How do we cultivate faithfulness to our commitments?

2 Kings 12:15 *No accounting was required from the construction supervisors, because they were honest and faithful workers.*

Daniel 6:4 *They couldn't find anything to criticize. He was faithful and honest.*
Cultivate faithfulness by being honest and trustworthy.

Deuteronomy 28:9 *If you obey the commands of the LORD your God and walk in his ways, the LORD will establish you as his holy people.*
Cultivate faithfulness by obeying God's word.

1 Timothy 3:12 *A deacon must be faithful to his wife.*
Cultivate faithfulness by keeping your promises.

PROMISES FROM GOD:
2 Thessalonians 3:3 *But the Lord is faithful; he will make you strong and guard you from the evil one.*

Hebrews 3:14 *For if we are faithful to the end . . . we will share in all that belongs to Christ.*

Communication

How can we best communicate with each other?

2 Corinthians 6:11-13 *Oh, dear Corinthian friends! We have spoken honestly with you. Our hearts are open to you. If there is a problem between us, it is not because of a lack of love on our part, but*

because you have withheld your love from us. I am talking now as I would to my own children. Open your hearts to us!

Our hearts need to be open if we are going to communicate effectively with one another.

1 Thessalonians 2:7 *As apostles of Christ we certainly had a right to make some demands of you, but we were as gentle among you as a mother feeding and caring for her own children.*

We need to have a gentle spirit in our communications.

Isaiah 50:4 *The Sovereign LORD has given me his words of wisdom, so that I know what to say to all these weary ones. Morning by morning he wakens me and opens my understanding to his will.*

We need to seek the Lord's wisdom and understanding.

Colossians 4:6 *Let your conversation be gracious and effective so that you will have the right answer for everyone.*

Ephesians 4:29 *Don't use foul or abusive language. Let everything you say be good and helpful, so that your words will be an encouragement to those who hear them.*

Our words should be gracious, effective, good, helpful, and encouraging to others.

2 Corinthians 1:13-14 *My letters have been straightforward, and there is nothing written between the lines and nothing you can't understand. I hope someday you will fully understand us, even if you don't fully understand us now.*
We need to be straightforward and clear in our communication so that we can help others understand.

2 Corinthians 6:4, 8 *In everything we do we try to show that we are true ministers of God. . . . We serve God whether people honor us or despise us, whether they slander us or praise us.*
We are called to communicate God and his ways through the way we live. What we do may speak much more eloquently than what we say.

How do we really listen?

Genesis 44:15 *"What were you trying to do?" Joseph demanded.*
Listening involves asking questions. Joseph asked this question, because his brothers' answer would reveal whether their hearts had changed.

Proverbs 15:32 *If you listen to correction, you grow in understanding.*
Listening involves being open to advice.

Proverbs 15:28 *The godly think before speaking.*
Listening often involves talking less.

What kinds of words should we speak?

Deuteronomy 6:4-7 *You must commit yourselves wholeheartedly to these commands I am giving you today. Repeat them again and again to your children. Talk about them when you are at home and when you are away on a journey, when you are lying down and when you are getting up again.*
Talk about God's commands on a continual basis.

Genesis 50:21 *And he spoke very kindly to them, reassuring them.*
Speak kind words to one another.

Job 16:5 *I would speak in a way that helps you. I would try to take away your grief.*

Ephesians 4:29 *Let everything you say be good and helpful, so that your words will be an encouragement to those who hear them.*
Use words which build up others.

Proverbs 15:4 *Gentle words bring life and health.*

Proverbs 25:15 *Patience can persuade a prince, and soft speech can crush strong opposition.*
Speak to one another with gentleness.

1 Peter 3:9 *Don't repay evil for evil. Don't retaliate when people say unkind things about you. Instead, pay them back with a blessing. That is what God wants you to do, and he will bless you for it.*

Use your words to bless one another, even when others' words injure you.

Z e c h a r i a h 8 : 1 6 *Tell the truth to each other. Render verdicts in your courts that are just and that lead to peace.*
Speak truthfully, in a way that promotes justice and peace.

PROMISE FROM GOD: P r o v e r b s 1 0 : 2 0
The words of the godly are like sterling silver.

Comparisons

What are the dangers of comparing ourselves to others?

J o h n 2 1 : 2 1 - 2 2 *Peter asked Jesus, "What about him, Lord?" Jesus replied, "If I want him to remain alive until I return, what is that to you? You follow me."*
Comparing ourselves to others takes our focus off Jesus.

L u k e 1 8 : 1 1 *The proud Pharisee stood by himself and prayed this prayer: "I thank you, God, that I am not a sinner like everyone else, especially like that tax collector over there!"*
Comparing ourselves to others may lead to false righteousness, thinking we are better than someone else.

How can we avoid the dangers of comparisons?

Romans 14:10, 12 *Why do you condemn another Christian? Why do you look down on another Christian? Remember, each of us will stand personally before the judgment seat of God. . . . Each of us will have to give a personal account to God.*
God looks at each of us individually. Your spouse or neighbor will give his or her own account to God. We will not account for one another.

2 Corinthians 13:5 *Examine yourselves to see if your faith is really genuine. Test yourselves. If you cannot tell that Jesus Christ is among you, it means you have failed the test.*

Galatians 6:4-5 *Be sure to do what you should, for then you will enjoy the personal satisfaction of having done your work well, and you won't need to compare yourself to anyone else. For we are each responsible for our own conduct.*
We are to examine our own faith and actions and do what we know we should.

Romans 12:15 *When others are happy, be happy with them. If they are sad, share their sorrow.*
We are to rejoice in our spouses' successes and not wish their successes were ours.

To whom should we compare ourselves?

1 Peter 1:15-16 *But now you must be holy in everything you do, just as God—who chose you to be his children—is holy. For he himself has said, "You must be holy because I am holy."*
We should compare ourselves only to Jesus. Are we living lives God would have us live? Are we moving toward the kind of faith and obedience he has called us to?

PROMISE FROM GOD: Jeremiah 10:6 *LORD, there is no one like you! For you are great, and your name is full of power.*

Compliment

see also Kindness *and* Manners

What is the importance of complimenting others? Why should we compliment each other?

Philippians 1:6 *I am sure that God, who began the good work within you, will continue his work until it is finally finished on that day when Christ Jesus comes back again.*

Colossians 2:5 *Though I am far away from you, my heart is with you. And I am very happy because you are living as you should and because of your strong faith in Christ.*

2 Thessalonians 1:4 *We proudly tell God's other churches about your endurance and faithfulness in all the persecutions and hardships you are suffering.*
Noticing spiritual growth in others can be encouraging to them.

2 Chronicles 30:22 *Hezekiah encouraged the Levites for the skill they displayed as they served the LORD.*
Verbally acknowledging another's skill or talent is a form of encouragement.

2 Corinthians 7:4 *I have the highest confidence in you, and my pride in you is great. You have greatly encouraged me; you have made me happy despite all our troubles.*
A compliment can be an expression of confidence.

Song of Songs 1:9-11 *What a lovely filly you are, my beloved one! How lovely are your cheeks, with your earrings setting them afire! How stately is your neck, accented with a long string of jewels. We will make earrings of gold for you and beads of silver.*

Song of Songs 4:7 *You are so beautiful, my beloved, so perfect in every part.*
A compliment can be an expression of love or appreciation.

PROMISE FROM GOD: 2 Corinthians 10:18
When people boast about themselves, it doesn't count for much. But when the Lord commends someone, that's different!

Compromise

When is compromise appropriate, and how do we effectively compromise?

Ezra 10:3-4 *We will follow the advice given by you and by the others who respect the commands of our God. We will obey the law of God. Take courage, for it is your duty to tell us how to proceed in setting things straight, and we will cooperate fully.*
It is never appropriate to compromise the will of God as revealed in Scripture. We must never give in if it means disobeying the Bible.

Romans 14:15 *And if another Christian is distressed by what you eat, you are not acting in love if you eat it. Don't let your eating ruin someone for whom Christ died.*
In order to maintain unity in the body of Christ, a Christian must be willing to avoid certain things. This may require compromising personal preferences—but never Christian convictions.

Romans 15:1 *We may know that these things make no difference, but we cannot just go ahead and do them to please ourselves. We must be considerate of the doubts and fears of those who think these things are wrong.*

We must be willing to compromise what pleases us for the sake of others.

Philippians 2:2 *Make me truly happy by agreeing wholeheartedly with each other, loving one another, and working together with one heart and purpose.*

Agreement may mean giving up something "I" want for the sake of what "we" want.

How should we respond when we are tempted to compromise God's ways?

1 Chronicles 22:13 *For if you carefully obey the laws and regulations that the LORD gave to Israel through Moses, you will be successful. Be strong and courageous; do not be afraid or lose heart!*

Careful obedience—backed by strength and courage—will help us resist temptation and remain steadfast.

1 Corinthians 16:13 *Be on guard. Stand true to what you believe. Be courageous. Be strong.*

When temptations come, the only appropriate response is to resist. God will give us the strength to do so.

PROMISE FROM GOD: Ephesians 6:11
Put on all of God's armor so that you will be able to stand firm against all strategies and tricks of the Devil.

Conceited

see **Ego**

Condemnation

Why shouldn't we judge others?

Romans 14:4, 10 *Who are you to condemn God's servants? They are responsible to the Lord, so let him tell them whether they are right or wrong.*

Remember, each of us will stand personally before the judgment seat of God.
We are each answerable to God. We don't have the right to condemn another.

Luke 6:41-42 *Why worry about a speck in your friend's eye when you have a log in your own? . . . First get rid of the log from your own eye; then perhaps you will see well enough to deal with the speck in your friend's eye.*

John 8:7, 9 *"All right, stone her. But let those who have never sinned throw the first stones!" . . .*

When the accusers heard this, they slipped away one by one, beginning with the oldest.
Our own sin disqualifies us from judging others. Only when we have recognized our sin and received God's forgiveness will we be ready to help another down the same path.

James 4:11 *Don't speak evil against each other, my dear brothers and sisters. If you criticize each other and condemn each other, then you are criticizing and condemning God's law. But you are not a judge who can decide whether the law is right or wrong. Your job is to obey it.*
Our job is not to judge but to obey God's ways.

How can we change our own condemning attitude?

2 Corinthians 5:17 *What this means is that those who become Christians become new persons. They are not the same anymore, for the old life is gone. A new life has begun!*
God gives us each a fresh start when we come to him—only he can change our hearts. If God is willing to give us a fresh start, shouldn't we be willing to do the same with our mate?

Psalm 139:23-24 *Search me, O God, and know my heart; test me and know my thoughts. Point out anything in me that offends you, and lead me along the path of everlasting life.*

We must ask God to examine our own lives, then respond to his findings and follow his ways.

Romans 14:10, 13 *Why do you condemn another Christian? Why do you look down on another Christian? . . . Don't condemn each other anymore. Decide instead to live in such a way that you will not put an obstacle in another Christian's path.*
Take the lead in setting a godly example for your mate. Demonstrate unconditional love.

Proverbs 3:3 *Never let loyalty and kindness get away from you! Wear them like a necklace; write them deep within your heart.*
We are to have hearts full of loyalty and kindness towards each other.

Ephesians 4:29 *Don't use foul or abusive language. Let everything you say be good and helpful, so that your words will be an encouragement to those who hear them.*
We are to speak helpful, encouraging words. If we do this consistently, what a difference it will make!

PROMISES FROM GOD: Psalm 34:22 *But the LORD will redeem those who serve him. Everyone who trusts in him will be freely pardoned.*

Romans 8:1-2 *So now there is no condemnation for those who belong to Christ Jesus. For the power of the life-giving Spirit has freed you through Christ Jesus from the power of sin that leads to death.*

Conflict

see also **Differences, Disagreement, and Quarreling**

What are some ways to resolve conflict?

Genesis 13:8 *Abram talked it over with Lot. "This arguing between our herdsmen has got to stop," he said.*
Solving conflict takes initiative; someone must make the first move. Abram gave Lot first choice, putting family peace above personal desires.

Genesis 26:21-22 *Isaac's men then dug another well, but again there was a fight over it. . . . He dug another well, and the local people finally left him alone.*
Solving conflict takes humility, persistence, and a preference for peace over personal victory.

1 Corinthians 6:7 *Why not just accept the injustice and leave it at that? Why not let yourselves be cheated?*
We might have to give up our rights to resolve a conflict of interests.

John 17:21 *My prayer for all of them is that they will be one, just as you and I are one, Father.*
We should join Jesus in praying for peace and unity with others—particularly our spouse.

Acts 15:37-39 *Barnabas . . . wanted to take along John Mark. But Paul disagreed strongly. . . .*

Their disagreement over this was so sharp that they separated.

Sometimes differences of opinion are so strong that no resolution seems possible, and a parting of ways is necessary. But even in these cases we can pray that God will bring good out of a painful experience.

2 Timothy 2:24-25 *The Lord's servants must not quarrel but must be kind to everyone. They must be patient with difficult people. They should gently teach those who oppose the truth.*

When someone disagrees with what we are saying, we should maintain a gracious, gentle, and patient attitude instead of becoming angry and defensive.

How do we keep conflict to a minimum?

Proverbs 26:17 *Yanking a dog's ears is as foolish as interfering in someone else's argument.*

It is sometimes tempting to jump into an argument in process and "solve it," but doing so often only heats up the issue.

Romans 12:18 *Do your part to live in peace with everyone, as much as possible.*

As Christ's ambassadors, we need to work actively for peace with others.

Ephesians 4:3 *Always keep yourselves united in the Holy Spirit, and bind yourselves together with peace.*
Spiritual unity and fellowship with God will help us bring unity and peace to our relationships.

PROMISE FROM GOD: Matthew 5:9 *God blesses those who work for peace, for they will be called the children of God.*

Confusion

How can we avoid confusion?

1 Kings 18:21 *Then Elijah stood in front of them and said, "How long are you going to waver between two opinions? If the LORD is God, follow him! But if Baal is God, then follow him!"*

Proverbs 3:5-6 *Trust in the LORD with all your heart; do not depend on your own understanding. Seek his will in all you do, and he will direct your paths.*
Trusting God and following his word give us focus and purpose.

How should we deal with life's confusion?

Psalm 94:19 *When doubts filled my mind, your comfort gave me renewed hope and cheer.*

Philippians 4:8-9 *Fix your thoughts on what is true and honorable and right. Think about things that are pure and lovely and admirable. Think about things that are excellent and worthy of praise. Keep putting into practice all you learned from me and heard from me and saw me doing, and the God of peace will be with you.*

Focusing our thoughts on the Lord gives us his comfort and peace—the answer to our confusion.

Psalm 75:3 *When the earth quakes and its people live in turmoil, I am the one who keeps its foundations firm.*

Isaiah 45:18 *For the LORD is God, and he created the heavens and earth and put everything in place. He made the world to be lived in, not to be a place of empty chaos. "I am the LORD," he says, "and there is no other."*

Trust God and recognize his sovereignty. God is the answer to our confusion.

Proverbs 20:24 *How can we understand the road we travel? It is the LORD who directs our steps.*

James 1:5 *If you need wisdom—if you want to know what God wants you to do—ask him, and he will gladly tell you. He will not resent your asking.*

Ask God for understanding. His wisdom will help us sort out the confusion.

Psalm 119:104-105 *Your commandments give me understanding; no wonder I hate every false way of life. Your word is a lamp for my feet and a light for my path.*
Look to Scripture for instruction and understanding.

John 16:13 *When the Spirit of truth comes, he will guide you into all truth. He will not be presenting his own ideas; he will be telling you what he has heard. He will tell you about the future.*
Be sensitive to the Holy Spirit. He gives the power and understanding to deal with confusion.

Hebrews 13:17 *Obey your spiritual leaders and do what they say. Their work is to watch over your souls, and they know they are accountable to God. Give them reason to do this joyfully and not with sorrow.*
Listen to wise teaching. You can learn what to do.

Ephesians 4:13-14 *We will be mature and full grown in the Lord, measuring up to the full stature of Christ. Then we will no longer be like children, forever changing our minds about what we believe.*

Hebrews 5:14 *Solid food is for those who are mature, who have trained themselves to recognize the difference between right and wrong and then do what is right.*
As we mature in Christ, we can learn to better handle things that confuse us.

PROMISES FROM GOD: Isaiah 45:18
For the LORD is God, and he created the heavens and earth and put everything in place. He made the world to be lived in, not to be a place of empty chaos. "I am the LORD," he says, "and there is no other."

1 Corinthians 14:33 *For God is not a God of disorder but of peace, as in all the other churches.*

Convictions

How do our convictions impact our relationships?

Philippians 1:6 *And I am sure that God, who began the good work within you, will continue his work until it is finally finished on that day when Christ Jesus comes back again.*
Realizing that we are each God's work in progress will help us be patient with each other as we continue to grow in faith.

2 Corinthians 6:14-15 *Don't team up with those who are unbelievers. How can goodness be a partner with wickedness? How can light live with darkness? What harmony can there be between Christ and the Devil? How can a believer be a partner with an unbeliever?*
We should seek to form our closest relationships with those who share our convictions.

Romans 14:1-6 *Accept Christians who are weak in faith, and don't argue with them about what they think is right or wrong. For instance, one person believes it is all right to eat anything. But another believer who has a sensitive conscience will eat only vegetables. Those who think it is all right to eat anything must not look down on those who won't. And those who won't eat certain foods must not condemn those who do, for God has accepted them. Who are you to condemn God's servants? They are responsible to the Lord, so let him tell them whether they are right or wrong. The Lord's power will help them do as they should.*

Having strong convictions does not mean being intolerant of or condemning one another. We are made in God's image. We are to trust God and study his word to help each of us know what is right and wrong by his standards and not our own.

How do we live out our convictions?

Hosea 14:9 *Let those who are wise understand these things. Let those who are discerning listen carefully. The paths of the LORD are true and right, and righteous people live by walking in them. But sinners stumble and fall along the way.*

We live out our convictions by listening closely to the Lord's wisdom.

Daniel 3:16-18 *Shadrach, Meshach, and Abednego replied, "O Nebuchadnezzar, we do not need to defend ourselves before you. If we are thrown into the blazing furnace, the God whom we serve is able to save us. He will rescue us from your power, Your Majesty. But even if he doesn't, Your Majesty can be sure that we will never serve your gods or worship the gold statue you have set up."*

Acts 5:29 *But Peter and the apostles replied, "We must obey God rather than human authority."*
We live out our convictions by keeping God in focus.

1 Thessalonians 2:2 *You know how badly we had been treated at Philippi just before we came to you and how much we suffered there. Yet our God gave us the courage to declare his Good News to you boldly, even though we were surrounded by many who opposed us.*

2 Corinthians 4:13 *But we continue to preach because we have the same kind of faith the psalmist had when he said, "I believed in God, and so I speak."*
We live out our convictions by the courage and faith which God gives us.

Daniel 1:8 *But Daniel made up his mind not to defile himself by eating the food and wine given to them by the king. He asked the chief official for permission to eat other things instead.*

Negotiating with those in charge can help us live out our convictions.

PROMISES FROM GOD:

2 Chronicles 19:9 *These were his instructions to them: "You must always act in the fear of the LORD, with integrity and with undivided hearts."*

Psalm 15:1-2 *Who may worship in your sanctuary, LORD? Who may enter your presence on your holy hill? Those who lead blameless lives and do what is right, speaking the truth from sincere hearts.*

Cooperation

see **Teamwork**

Counsel/Counselors

How are we to counsel others?

Galatians 6:1 *Dear friends, if a Christian is overcome by some sin, you who are godly should gently and humbly help that person back onto the right path. And be careful not to fall into the same temptation yourself.*
Our counsel should be gentle and humble.

Colossians 3:16 *Let the words of Christ, in all their richness, live in your hearts and make you wise. Use his words to teach and counsel each other.*
We should counsel others using the words of Scripture.

Ezekiel 3:20-21 *If good people turn bad and don't listen to my warning, they will die. If you did not warn them of the consequences, then they will die in their sins. Their previous good deeds won't help them, and I will hold you responsible, demanding your blood for theirs. But if you warn them and they repent, they will live, and you will have saved your own life, too.*

Hebrews 3:13 *You must warn each other every day, as long as it is called "today," so that none of you will be deceived by sin and hardened against God.*
We should warn those who are in sin of the consequences that await them and encourage them to repent, turning to God to forgive and save them.

1 Thessalonians 5:14 *Brothers and sisters, we urge you to warn those who are lazy. Encourage those who are timid. Take tender care of those who are weak. Be patient with everyone.*
Our counsel should address the need of the person, but in every case we must give our counsel patiently and in love.

Romans 14:19 *So then, let us aim for harmony in the church and try to build each other up.*

Romans 15:2 *We should please others. If we do what helps them, we will build them up in the Lord.*

1 Thessalonians 5:11 *So encourage each other and build each other up, just as you are already doing.*

Hebrews 10:24 *Think of ways to encourage one another to outbursts of love and good deeds.*
Our counsel should aim at encouraging others, building them up, and fostering harmony in the church.

How should we respond to wise counsel?

Proverbs 1:7 *Only fools despise wisdom and discipline.*

Proverbs 9:9 *Teach the wise, and they will be wiser. Teach the righteous, and they will learn more.*

Proverbs 13:10 *Those who take advice are wise.*
We should listen to wise counsel and do what we are advised to do. Not doing so is an indication of stubbornness and pride.

PROMISES FROM GOD: Psalm 32:8
The LORD says, "I will guide you along the best pathway for your life. I will advise you and watch over you."

Psalm 73:24 *You will keep on guiding me with your counsel, leading me to a glorious destiny.*

Criticism

How should we respond to criticism? How do we evaluate whether it is constructive or destructive?

Proverbs 12:16-18 *A wise person stays calm when insulted. An honest witness tells the truth; a false witness tells lies. Some people make cutting remarks, but the words of the wise bring healing.*
If you are criticized, stay calm and don't lash back. Evaluate whether the criticism is coming from a person with a reputation for truth or lies. Ask yourself if the criticism is meant to help or to hurt.

Ecclesiastes 7:5 *It is better to be criticized by a wise person than to be praised by a fool!*
Measure criticism by the reputation of the person who is giving it.

1 Corinthians 4:4 *My conscience is clear, but that isn't what matters. It is the Lord himself who will examine me and decide.*
Always work to maintain a clear conscience before God. This allows you to shrug off criticism you know is unjustified.

How do we administer criticism when we feel it must be given?

John 8:7 *Let those who have never sinned throw the first stones!*

Romans 2:1 *When you say they are wicked and should be punished, you are condemning yourself, for you do these very same things.*

Matthew 7:5 *First get rid of the log from your own eye; then perhaps you will see well enough to deal with the speck in your friend's eye.*
Before criticizing another, especially your spouse, take an inventory of your own sins and shortcomings so that you can approach the person with understanding and humility.

PROMISE FROM GOD: Proverbs 15:31 *If you listen to constructive criticism, you will be at home among the wise.*

Dating

see **Friendship** *and* **Romance**

Decisions

How can we be more decisive?

Philippians 2:13 *For God is working in you, giving you the desire to obey him and the power to do what pleases him.*

Psalm 25:4, 12 *Show me the path where I should walk, O LORD; point out the right road for me to follow. . . . Who are those who fear the LORD? He will show them the path they should choose.*

Isaiah 50:7 *Because the Sovereign LORD helps me, I will not be dismayed. Therefore, I have set my face like a stone, determined to do his will. And I know that I will triumph.*

Ask God to give you wisdom, perspective, and a desire to obey him. Knowing God's will and being committed to doing it help us to be more decisive.

Psalm 119:5-11 *Oh, that my actions would consistently reflect your principles! Then I will not be disgraced when I compare my life with your commands. When I learn your righteous laws, I will thank you by living as I should! I will obey your principles. Please don't give up on me! How can a young person stay pure? By obeying your word and following its rules. I have tried my best to find you—don't let me wander from your commands. I*

have hidden your word in my heart, that I might not sin against you.
Knowing God's word helps us to know what to do.

Psalm 119:8, 57 *I will obey your principles. Please don't give up on me! . . . LORD, you are mine! I promise to obey your words!*

Psalm 119:30 *I have chosen to be faithful; I have determined to live by your laws.*
Choosing to always obey God helps us to be decisive in both large and small decisions.

Hebrews 11:8 *It was by faith that Abraham obeyed when God called him to leave home and go to another land that God would give him as his inheritance. He went without knowing where he was going.*
Having faith in God will help us be decisive because we know that he holds the future. We don't have to know where we are going when we are going with God.

What are some principles of good decision making?

1 John 5:14 *We can be confident that he will listen to us whenever we ask him for anything in line with his will.*
Ask God for guidance—he is glad to help you follow his will.

88

Psalm 119:98 *Your commands make me wiser than my enemies, for your commands are my constant guide.*

Romans 2:18 *Yes, you know what he wants; you know right from wrong because you have been taught his law.*
God's word gives us wisdom to know what God wants. Divine common sense will help us make good decisions.

Luke 6:12-13 *Jesus went to a mountain to pray, and he prayed to God all night. At daybreak he called together all of his disciples and chose twelve of them to be apostles.*
Do as Jesus did and saturate your major decisions with prayer.

Proverbs 12:15 *Fools think they need no advice, but the wise listen to others.*

Psalm 37:30 *The godly offer good counsel; they know what is right from wrong.*
Listen to godly counsel.

Proverbs 18:15 *Intelligent people are always open to new ideas. In fact, they look for them.*
Be open to new ideas.

Proverbs 18:13 *What a shame, what folly, to give advice before listening to the facts!*
Make sure you have all the facts.

How do we know if we've made a good decision?

Galatians 5:22-23 *But when the Holy Spirit controls our lives, he will produce this kind of fruit in us: love, joy, peace, patience, kindness, goodness, faithfulness, gentleness, and self-control.*
You know you've made a good decision when your decision produces good results.

Hebrews 5:14 *Solid food is for those who have trained themselves to recognize the differences between right and wrong, and then do what is right.*
You will more consistently make good decisions if you spend consistent time in God's word and act upon its principles.

PROMISES FROM GOD: Proverbs 3:6 *Seek his will in all you do, and he will direct your paths.*

James 1:5-8 *If you need wisdom—if you want to know what God wants you to do—ask him, and he will gladly tell you.*

Dependence/Dependability

For what things should we depend only on God?

Romans 5:6 *When we were utterly helpless, Christ came at just the right time and died for us sinners.*

John 3:36 *And all who believe in God's Son have eternal life. Those who don't obey the Son will never experience eternal life, but the wrath of God remains upon them.*
We should depend on God alone for our eternal salvation.

2 Thessalonians 3:3 *But the Lord is faithful; he will make you strong and guard you from the evil one.*

Ephesians 6:10-11 *Be strong with the Lord's mighty power. Put on all of God's armor so that you will be able to stand firm against all strategies and tricks of the Devil.*
We should depend on God alone for our strength and power against evil.

Isaiah 41:10 *Don't be afraid, for I am with you. Do not be dismayed, for I am your God. I will strengthen you. I will help you. I will uphold you with my victorious right hand.*

Matthew 28:20 *"I am with you always, even to the end of the age."*
We should depend on God alone for God's continual presence.

How do we depend on God?

John 6:29 *Jesus told them, "This is what God wants you to do: Believe in the one he has sent."*
We depend on God by believing in his Son.

Psalm 5:2 *Listen to my cry for help, my King and my God, for I will never pray to anyone but you.*

Psalm 119:147 *I rise early, before the sun is up; I cry out for help and put my hope in your words.*
We depend on God by praying to him.

Mark 10:14-15 *"Let the children come to me. Don't stop them! For the Kingdom of God belongs to such as these. I assure you, anyone who doesn't have their kind of faith will never get into the Kingdom of God."*

Luke 23:40-42 *But the other criminal protested, "Don't you fear God even when you are dying? We deserve to die for our evil deeds, but this man hasn't done anything wrong." Then he said, "Jesus, remember me when you come into your Kingdom."*
We depend on God by placing childlike faith in Jesus.

Who else should we depend on in addition to God?

Galatians 6:2 *Share each other's troubles and problems, and in this way obey the law of Christ.*

Ecclesiastes 4:9-10 *Two people can accomplish more than twice as much as one; they get a better return for their labor. If one person falls, the other can reach out and help.*
We are right to depend on others for friendship, prayer, ministry, and growth.

How can we become more dependable?

Proverbs 25:19 *Putting confidence in an unreliable person is like chewing with a toothache or walking on a broken foot.*

Proverbs 11:13 *A gossip goes around revealing secrets, but those who are trustworthy can keep a confidence.*
We can become more dependable in our relationships by being trustworthy.

Ephesians 6:5-8 *Slaves, obey your earthly masters with deep respect and fear. Serve them sincerely as you would serve Christ. Work hard, but not just to please your masters when they are watching. As slaves of Christ, do the will of God with all your heart. Work with enthusiasm, as though you were working for the Lord rather than for people. Remember that the Lord will reward each one of us for the good we do, whether we are slaves or free.*
We can become more dependable in our work by showing respect to those in authority, by working hard, and by doing it with a positive attitude.

PROMISE FROM GOD: Jeremiah 17:7-8 *But blessed are those who trust in the LORD and have made the LORD their hope and confidence. They are like trees planted along a riverbank, with roots that reach deep into the water. Such trees are not bothered by the heat or worried by long months of drought. Their leaves stay green, and they go right on producing delicious fruit.*

Differences

see also **Conflict, Disagreement, and Quarreling**

How does God want us to deal with our differences?

Deuteronomy 10:19 *You, too, must show love to foreigners, for you yourselves were once foreigners in the land of Egypt.*

God wants us to show his love toward those who are different from us, whether they are different in race or just personality.

Psalm 133:1-3 *How wonderful it is, how pleasant, when brothers live together in harmony! For harmony is as precious as the fragrant anointing oil. . . . Harmony is as refreshing as the dew. . . . And the LORD has pronounced his blessing, even life forevermore.*

God wants us to live in harmony despite our differences.

Proverbs 17:14 *Beginning a quarrel is like opening a floodgate, so drop the matter before a dispute breaks out.*

1 Corinthians 1:10 *Stop arguing among yourselves. Let there be real harmony so there won't be divisions in the church. . . . Be of one mind, united in thought and purpose.*

Even if we disagree with another, we should

avoid arguing and causing division. We should look to find ways to resolve our differences peaceably.

Ephesians 2:14 *Christ himself has made peace between us Jews and you Gentiles by making us all one people. He has broken down the wall of hostility that used to separate us.*

Ephesians 4:3 *Always keep yourselves united in the Holy Spirit, and bind yourselves together with peace.* God puts very different people together in the church, and then unites them through the Holy Spirit. God often puts very different people together in marriage so that their gifts can complement each other.

Can our differences help us be stronger?

Proverbs 27:17 *As iron sharpens iron, a friend sharpens a friend.*

Romans 12:5 *So it is with Christ's body. We are all parts of his one body, and each of us has different work to do. And since we are all one body in Christ, we belong to each other, and each of us needs all the others.* People with different gifts and perspectives can make one another stronger. All kinds of instruments are needed in an orchestra. A strong marriage is one where a variety of gifts are brought to the partnership.

PROMISE FROM GOD:
2 Corinthians 13:11 *Live in harmony and peace. Then the God of love and peace will be with you.*

Disagreement

see also **Conflict, Differences,** *and* **Quarreling**

How do we best handle disagreements in our marriage?

1 Corinthians 13:4-5 *Love is patient and kind. Love is not jealous or boastful or proud or rude. Love does not demand its own way. Love is not irritable, and it keeps no record of when it has been wronged.*

Colossians 3:14 *The most important piece of clothing you must wear is love. Love is what binds us all together in perfect harmony.*

Proverbs 10:12 *Hatred stirs up quarrels, but love covers all offenses.*
We can best handle marital disagreements by showing love rather than trying to get even.

Romans 15:5 *May God, who gives this patience and encouragement, help you live in complete harmony with each other—each with the attitude of Christ Jesus toward the other.*
We can best handle marital disagreements with God's help and perspective toward our mate.

Proverbs 13:10 *Pride leads to arguments; those who take advice are wise.*
We can best handle marital disagreements with humility, recognizing that our spouse may be right.

Mark 3:25 *A home divided against itself is doomed.*

Amos 3:3 *Can two people walk together without agreeing on the direction?*
We can best handle marital disagreements by remembering the importance of unity, which is far better than the hollow satisfaction of winning an argument.

Proverbs 15:1 *A gentle answer turns away wrath, but harsh words stir up anger.*
We can best handle marital disagreements with gentle words to one another. We need to keep our tempers from flaring and to avoid saying things we'll regret later.

How do we best handle disagreements in our families?

Genesis 13:8 *Then Abram talked it over with Lot. "This arguing between our herdsmen has got to stop," he said. "After all, we are close relatives!"*
We can best handle family disagreements by maturely taking the initiative and placing family over personal desires.

Proverbs 15:1 *A gentle answer turns away wrath, but harsh words stir up anger.*

We can best handle family disagreements by using gentle words with one another.

How should we disagree?

Proverbs 17:27 *A truly wise person uses few words; a person with understanding is even-tempered.*

Proverbs 15:1 *A gentle answer turns away wrath, but harsh words stir up anger.*
We should wisely choose few and gentle words. We are to be understanding and even-tempered. The goal is not to win the argument, but to exercise God's love and justice.

PROMISE FROM GOD: James 3:18 *Those who are peacemakers will plant seeds of peace and reap a harvest of goodness.*

Discouragement

see also Encouragement

How can we handle discouragement?

1 Peter 5:8-9 *Watch out for attacks from the Devil. . . . Take a firm stand against him, and be strong in your faith. Remember that Christians all over the world are going through the same kind of suffering you are.*

Discouragement makes us feel sorry for ourselves. We must guard against thinking we are the only ones who are going through troubles. Instead, we can take heart in the knowledge that we are not alone.

1 Samuel 1:10 *Hannah was in deep anguish, crying bitterly as she prayed to the LORD.*
Prayer is the first step we must take when discouraged.

2 Chronicles 20:15 *Don't be discouraged by this mighty army, for the battle is not yours, but God's.*
It would have been easy for the people of Judah to see only the vast enemy army and not God standing over it. We must realize that God will fight on our behalf and help us succeed as we trust in him.

PROMISES FROM GOD: Joshua 1:9 *Be strong and courageous! Do not be afraid or discouraged. For the LORD your God is with you wherever you go.*

Galatians 6:9 *Don't get discouraged and give up, for we will reap a harvest of blessing at the appropriate time.*

Dissatisfaction

see also **Happiness** *and* **Satisfaction**

What are the dangers of dissatisfaction?

Ezekiel 16:28-29 *You have prostituted yourselves with the Assyrians, too. It seems you can never find enough new lovers! And after your prostitution there, you still were not satisfied. You added to your lovers by embracing that great merchant land of Babylonia—but you still weren't satisfied!*
Dissatisfaction usually breeds even greater dissatisfaction. The solution to dissatisfaction is to practice faithfulness to God, to our mate, and to the commitments we have made.

Proverbs 14:30 *A relaxed attitude lengthens life; jealousy rots it away.*
Dissatisfaction can lead to jealousy, bitterness, and a shorter life. Being satisfied with what we have helps us relax and enjoy the life God has given us.

Psalm 106:25 *Instead, they grumbled in their tents and refused to obey the LORD.*
Dissatisfaction with what you have often leads to disobedience.

1 Corinthians 10:10 *And don't grumble as some of them did, for that is why God sent his angel of death to destroy them.*

James 5:9 *Don't grumble about each other, my brothers and sisters, or God will judge you. For look! The great Judge is coming. He is standing at the door!* Dissatisfaction with what you have can lead to grumbling, nagging, and complaining.

How do we respond to dissatisfaction in our marriages?

Malachi 2:14-16 *You cry out, "Why has the LORD abandoned us?" I'll tell you why! Because the LORD witnessed the vows you and your wife made to each other on your wedding day when you were young. But you have been disloyal to her, though she remained your faithful companion, the wife of your marriage vows. Didn't the LORD make you one with your wife? In body and spirit you are his. And what does he want? Godly children from your union. So guard yourself; remain loyal to the wife of your youth. "For I hate divorce!" says the LORD, the God of Israel. "It is as cruel as putting on a victim's bloodstained coat," says the LORD Almighty. "So guard yourself; always remain loyal to your wife."*
Loyally fulfilling our vows to our spouse brings a satisfying marriage—not only physically satisfying, but spiritually satisfying. Loyalty brings the satisfaction that comes with being obedient to God and building trust in your relationship. Trust and unconditional love are the keys to lasting satisfaction.

Proverbs 5:15-18 *Drink water from your own well—share your love only with your wife. Why spill the water of your springs in public, having sex with just anyone? You should reserve it for yourselves. Don't share it with strangers. Let your wife be a fountain of blessing for you. Rejoice in the wife of your youth. She is a loving doe, a graceful deer. Let her breasts satisfy you always. May you always be captivated by her love.*

God planned for your mate to be a fountain of blessing. If we drink from other wells, how then can God satisfy us with the fountain he gave us? Stay true—dissatisfaction will wither, and satisfaction will well up.

1 Corinthians 13:7 *Love never gives up, never loses faith, is always hopeful, and endures through every circumstance.*

Commitment is the glue that binds a marriage together. Love persists through all circumstances. It is truly satisfying to experience that.

PROMISES FROM GOD: Acts 17:24-25 *He is the God who made the world and everything in it. . . . He satisfies every need there is.*

Divorce

What does the Bible say about divorce?

Malachi 2:14-16 *You cry out, "Why has the LORD abandoned us?" I'll tell you why! Because the LORD witnessed the vows you and your wife made to each other on your wedding day. . . . But you have been disloyal to her, though she remained your faithful companion. . . . Didn't the LORD make you one with your wife? In body and spirit you are his. . . . So guard yourself; remain loyal to the wife of your youth. "For I hate divorce!" says the LORD.*
Divorce is wrong because it is the breaking of a binding commitment. One or both spouses have made a conscious decision to be unfaithful.

Matthew 19:3 *Some Pharisees came and tried to trap him . . . "Should a man be allowed to divorce his wife for any reason?"*
The Old Testament provided specific rules concerning divorce and allowed limited remarriage in special cases (Deuteronomy 24:1-4). At the same time it was clear that divorce is not God's intention (Malachi 2:14-16). The New Testament also makes it clear that divorce is wrong (Matthew 5:31-32; 1 Corinthians 7:10-11), while allowing for limited exceptions as Jesus mentions in this passage.

What are some ways to prevent divorce?

Ephesians 5:24-25 *As the church submits to Christ, so you wives must submit to your husbands in everything. And you husbands must love your wives with the same love Christ showed the church.*

1 Thessalonians 5:11 *Encourage each other and build each other up.*
Couples who love each other with the kind of love Christ showed when he died for us, who seek to please one another, and who build one another up —these are the couples who will likely remain together in a happy marriage. The format is simple, but the fulfillment takes some doing!

Will God forgive me if I do get divorced?

Psalm 103:3 *He forgives all my sins.*

1 John 1:9 *But if we confess our sins to him, he is faithful and just to forgive us and to cleanse us from every wrong.*

Ephesians 3:18 *And may you have the power to understand . . . how wide, how long, how high, and how deep his love really is.*
No sin is beyond God's forgiveness, and nothing others do against us can separate us from God's unconditional love. But it is playing with fire to disobey God's clear commands, anticipating future forgiveness.

How do I deal with the bitterness I feel?

Hebrews 12:15 *Watch out that no bitter root of unbelief rises up among you, for whenever it springs up, many are corrupted by its poison.*
You may have been hurt badly, you may have been treated unjustly, or you may have been humiliated, but if you allow your bitterness to fester and grow, it will overshadow all you do and render you useless for effectively serving God. You must forgive so that God's Holy Spirit can continue to work in your life and help you start anew.

PROMISE FROM GOD: Ephesians 3:18 *May you have the power to understand . . . how wide, how long, how high, and how deep his love really is.*

Ego

How does ego affect relationships?

Proverbs 13:10 *Pride leads to arguments.*

Philippians 2:3 *Don't be selfish; don't live to make a good impression on others. Be humble, thinking of others as better than yourself.*

Luke 14:7-8, 11 *When Jesus noticed that all who had come to the dinner were trying to sit near the head of the table, he gave them this advice: "If you are invited to a wedding feast, don't always head for the best seat. . . . For the proud will be humbled, but the humble will be honored."*

Proverbs 16:19 *It is better to live humbly with the poor than to share plunder with the proud.*
Pride makes us argumentative and selfish, pressing for what we want at the expense of others. Why? Proud people falsely believe they are better than others. The conceited person loses the godly quality of serving others, depriving them of great joy.

2 Peter 2:18 *They brag about themselves with empty, foolish boasting. With lustful desire as their bait, they lure back into sin those who have just escaped from such wicked living.*
Conceited people—thinking only about their own desires—can tempt others to sin.

1 Corinthians 13:4 *Love is patient and kind. Love is not jealous or boastful or proud.*
Conceited people are not loving people, except that they love themselves.

1 Timothy 6:3-4 *Some false teachers may deny these things, but these are the sound, wholesome teachings of the Lord Jesus Christ, and they are the foundation for a godly life. Anyone who teaches anything different is both conceited and ignorant.*
Conceited people resist biblical truth when it contradicts what they want to believe.

What is the difference between ego and confidence?

Jeremiah 9:23-24 *This is what the LORD says: "Let not the wise man gloat in his wisdom, or the mighty man in his might, or the rich man in his riches. Let them boast in this alone: that they truly know me and understand that I am the LORD who is just and righteous, whose love is unfailing, and that I delight in these things. I, the LORD, have spoken!"*

Romans 15:17 *So it is right for me to be enthusiastic about all Christ Jesus has done through me in my service to God.*
Ego is trust in self—often to the exclusion of God. Our confidence should be that God is with us.

How do we keep from being egotistical?

Psalm 31:23 *Love the LORD, all you faithful ones! For the LORD protects those who are loyal to him, but he harshly punishes all who are arrogant.*
We are to love the Lord God and be loyal to him. This means putting him first and not ourselves.

1 Corinthians 1:31 *As the Scriptures say, "The person who wishes to boast should boast only of what the Lord has done."*
We are to praise what God has done, not what we have done. This means always acknowledging his work in our lives.

Philippians 2:3 *Don't be selfish; don't live to make a good impression on others. Be humble, thinking of others as better than yourself.*
We are to have a humble estimation of ourselves. This means realizing that we need others and God to help us accomplish our goals.

1 Peter 5:5-6 *You younger men, accept the authority of the elders. And all of you, serve each other in humility, for "God sets himself against the proud, but he shows favor to the humble." So humble yourselves under the mighty power of God, and in his good time he will honor you.*

Galatians 6:3 *If you think you are too important to help someone in need, you are only fooling yourself. You are really a nobody.*
We are to humbly serve one another. This means seeing value and beauty in the lives of others.

PROMISES FROM GOD: Psalm 69:32 *The humble will see their God at work and be glad. Let all who seek God's help live in joy.*

Isaiah 29:19 *The humble will be filled with fresh joy from the LORD.*

Empathy

How does empathy impact relationships?

1 Peter 3:8 *Finally, all of you should be of one mind, full of sympathy toward each other, loving one another with tender hearts and humble minds.*

Exodus 23:9 *Do not oppress the foreigners living among you. You know what it is like to be a foreigner. Remember your own experience in the land of Egypt.* Empathy helps us to be attentive to others and their needs. True empathy moves us to action.

How can we be more empathetic?

2 Corinthians 1:3-4 *He comforts us in all our troubles so that we can comfort others. When others are troubled, we will be able to give them the same comfort God has given us.*
God, the source of all mercy and comfort, will help us be more empathetic as we minister to others.

1 Peter 1:22 *Now you can have sincere love for each other as brothers and sisters because you were cleansed from your sins when you accepted the truth of the Good News. So see to it that you really do love each other intensely with all your hearts.*

1 John 3:18 *Dear children, let us stop just saying we love each other; let us really show it by our actions.* When we have accepted the truth of the Good News and recognized our own need for God's compassion, we should be moved to act in empathy toward others.

Galatians 6:2 *Share each other's troubles and problems, and in this way obey the law of Christ.*

Hebrews 13:3 *Don't forget about those in prison. Suffer with them as though you were there yourself. Share the sorrow of those being mistreated, as though you feel their pain in your own bodies.*

1 Corinthians 12:26 *If one part suffers, all the parts suffer with it, and if one part is honored, all the parts are glad.*
We should be more than concerned about others' troubles and problems—we are to be emotionally involved in each other's lives.

How can we show empathy to others?

Hebrews 10:33 *Sometimes you were exposed to public ridicule and were beaten, and sometimes you helped others who were suffering the same things.*
We can show empathy by feeling deeply what another person is going through.

Luke 10:36-37 *"Now which of these three would you say was a neighbor to the man who was attacked by bandits?" Jesus asked. The man replied, "The one*

who showed him mercy." Then Jesus said, "Yes, now go and do the same."
We can show empathy by helping a person in need.

PROMISE FROM GOD:
2 Corinthians 1:3-5 *All praise to the God and Father of our Lord Jesus Christ. He is the source of every mercy and the God who comforts us. He comforts us in all our troubles so that we can comfort others. . . . You can be sure that the more we suffer for Christ, the more God will shower us with his comfort through Christ.*

Encouragement

see also Discouragement

How does God encourage us?

1 Kings 19:4-6 *Then he went on alone into the desert, traveling all day. He sat down under a solitary broom tree and prayed that he might die. "I have had enough, LORD," he said. . . . But as he was sleeping, an angel touched him and told him, "Get up and eat!" He looked around and saw some bread baked on hot stones and a jar of water!*
God encourages us by meeting our needs in his timing.

Psalm 138:3 *When I pray, you answer me; you encourage me by giving me the strength I need.*
God gives us strength when we ask.

Psalm 119:25, 28 *I lie in the dust, completely discouraged; revive me by your word. . . . I weep with grief; encourage me by your word.*

Romans 15:4 *The Scriptures . . . give us hope and encouragement as we wait patiently for God's promises.*
God has given his written word to give us hope and encouragement.

Matthew 9:2 *Some people brought to him a paralyzed man on a mat. Seeing their faith, Jesus said to the paralyzed man, "Take heart, son! Your sins are forgiven."*

Matthew 9:22 *Jesus turned around and said to her, "Daughter, be encouraged! Your faith has made you well." And the woman was healed at that moment.*
God encourages us by forgiving our sins.

Hebrews 12:5, 10-11 *And have you entirely forgotten the encouraging words God spoke to you, his children? He said, "My child, don't ignore it when the Lord disciplines you, and don't be discouraged when he corrects you." . . . God's discipline is always right and good for us because it means we will share in his*

holiness. . . . Afterward there will be a quiet harvest of right living for those who are trained in this way.
Even when God disciplines us, it can be an encouragement to know he is working for our ultimate good.

How do we build each other up?

Zechariah 7:9 *Judge fairly and honestly, and show mercy and kindness to one another.*

1 Peter 3:8 *All of you should be of one mind, full of sympathy toward each other, loving one another with tender hearts and humble minds.*

Ephesians 4:2 *Be humble and gentle. Be patient with each other, making allowance for each other's faults because of your love.*
We can build others up by treating them with honesty, mercy, humility, gentleness, and tenderness.

Romans 15:2 *We should please others. If we do what helps them, we will build them up in the Lord.*
Considering others' welfare helps us build them up in Christ.

Ephesians 4:32 *Instead, be kind to each other, tenderhearted, forgiving one another, just as God through Christ has forgiven you.*
Forgiving others helps us build them up.

Hebrews 12:14 *Try to live in peace with everyone, and seek to live a clean and holy life, for those who are not holy will not see the Lord.*

Romans 14:19 *So then, let us aim for harmony in the church and try to build each other up.*
Making peace in our relationships with others helps build them up.

How can we be an encouragement to others?

1 Samuel 23:16 *Jonathan went to find David and encouraged him to stay strong in his faith in God.*
We can encourage friends to keep a close relationship with God.

Ephesians 4:29 *Don't use foul or abusive language. Let everything you say be good and helpful, so that your words will be an encouragement to those who hear them.*
We can encourage others by making sure everything we say is kind and uplifting.

Philippians 1:6 *And I am sure that God, who began the good work within you, will continue his work until it is finally finished.*
Remind people what God wants to do for them and through them.

2 Chronicles 30:22 *Hezekiah encouraged the Levites for the skill they displayed as they served the LORD.*

Compliment others for a job well done.

Proverbs 15:30 *A cheerful look brings joy to the heart; good news makes for good health.*
Smile!

PROMISE FROM GOD:
2 Thessalonians 2:16-17 *May our Lord Jesus Christ and God our Father . . . comfort your hearts and give you strength in every good thing you do and say.*

Energy

Where should we spend our energies?

Mark 12:30 *And you must love the Lord your God with all your heart, all your soul, all your mind, and all your strength.*
Loving God and obeying him should be the focus of our energies.

Matthew 6:31-33 *So don't worry about having enough food or drink or clothing. . . . Your heavenly Father . . . will give you all you need from day to day if you live for him and make the Kingdom of God your primary concern.*
We should spend our energy spreading the rule of God in people's lives.

115

1 Timothy 4:7 *Spend your time and energy in training yourself for spiritual fitness.*
We should spend our energy training to serve God.

Philippians 3:13 *No, dear brothers and sisters, I am still not all I should be, but I am focusing all my energies on this one thing: Forgetting the past and looking forward to what lies ahead.*
We should focus our energy on the future.

Acts 20:24 *But my life is worth nothing unless I use it for doing the work assigned me by the Lord Jesus—the work of telling others the Good News about God's wonderful kindness and love.*

1 Corinthians 15:58 *So, my dear brothers and sisters, be strong and steady, always enthusiastic about the Lord's work, for you know that nothing you do for the Lord is ever useless.*
Focusing our energies on what God has given us to do gives our lives worth and satisfaction.

2 Corinthians 12:15 *I will gladly spend myself and all I have for your spiritual good.*
We should spend our time and energy on others' spiritual well-being.

How can we find more energy?

Ephesians 6:7 *Work with enthusiasm, as though you were working for the Lord rather than for people.*
Doing our work for the Lord means working to

please him, not just people. This stimulates us to work with greater enthusiasm and energy.

Galatians 6:9 *So don't get tired of doing what is good. Don't get discouraged and give up, for we will reap a harvest of blessing at the appropriate time.* Realizing that our efforts will be rewarded helps us to work with sustained energy.

Genesis 2:2 *On the seventh day, having finished his task, God rested from all his work.*

Exodus 20:8-10 *Remember to observe the Sabbath day by keeping it holy. Six days a week are set apart for your daily duties and regular work, but the seventh day is a day of rest dedicated to the LORD your God.*

Psalm 127:2 *It is useless for you to work so hard from early morning until late at night, anxiously working for food to eat; for God gives rest to his loved ones.*
Setting aside times of rest renews us mentally, emotionally, and physically, giving us more energy for the work ahead.

How can we help others operating on low energy?

Colossians 1:11 *We also pray that you will be strengthened with his glorious power so that you will have all the patience and endurance you need. May you be filled with joy,*

117

We can pray that God will strengthen them.

Isaiah 50:4 *The Sovereign LORD has given me his words of wisdom, so that I know what to say to all these weary ones. Morning by morning he wakens me and opens my understanding to his will.*
We can ask God to give us wisdom and understanding to know what we can say to strengthen them.

PROMISE FROM GOD: Isaiah 40:29-31 *He gives power to those who are tired and worn out; he offers strength to the weak. Even youths will become exhausted, and young men will give up. But those who wait on the LORD will find new strength. They will fly high on wings like eagles. They will run and not grow weary. They will walk and not faint.*

Envy

see also Jealousy

What is the result of envy?

Job 5:2 *Surely resentment destroys the fool, and jealousy kills the simple.*

Psalm 37:8 *Stop your anger! Turn from your rage! Do not envy others—it only leads to harm.*

Proverbs 14:30 *A relaxed attitude lengthens life; jealousy rots it away.*

Unchecked envy will eventually destroy your life and harm others.

What do we do about our feelings of envy?

Psalm 37:1, 7 *Don't worry about the wicked. Don't envy those who do wrong. . . . Be still in the presence of the LORD, and wait patiently for him to act.*

Proverbs 24:19-20 *Do not fret because of evildoers; don't envy the wicked. For the evil have no future; their light will be snuffed out.*
Why envy sinners? They will only receive God's judgment. We should wait patiently for God to act in our lives in the way that is best.

John 21:20-22 *Peter turned around and saw the disciple Jesus loved following them—the one who had leaned over to Jesus during supper and asked, "Lord, who among us will betray you?" Peter asked Jesus, "What about him, Lord?" Jesus replied, "If I want him to remain alive until I return, what is that to you? You follow me."*
Each of us has a unique role to fulfill. Rather than worrying about others' position or advantages, trust God to work out his plan in you.

PROMISE FROM GOD: Proverbs 12:12 *Thieves are jealous of each other's loot, while the godly bear their own fruit.*

Equality

How is there equality in marriage?

Genesis 2:21-23 *So the LORD God caused Adam to fall into a deep sleep. He took one of Adam's ribs and closed up the place from which he had taken it. Then the LORD God made a woman from the rib and brought her to Adam. "At last!" Adam exclaimed. "She is part of my own flesh and bone! She will be called 'woman,' because she was taken out of a man."*

1 Corinthians 11:3,11-12 *A man is responsible to Christ, a woman is responsible to her husband, and Christ is responsible to God. . . . But in relationships among the Lord's people, women are not independent of men, and men are not independent of women. For although the first woman came from man, all men have been born from women ever since, and everything comes from God.*

Ephesians 5:22, 25 *You wives will submit to your husbands as you do to the Lord. . . . And you husbands must love your wives with the same love Christ showed the church. He gave up his life for her.*

1 Corinthians 7:4 *The wife gives authority over her body to her husband, and the husband also gives authority over his body to his wife.*

1 Peter 3:7 *You husbands must give honor to your wives. Treat her with understanding as you live together. She may be weaker than you are, but she is your equal partner in God's gift of new life.*
Husbands and wives are created equal. Although God has assigned different roles and responsibilities to husbands and wives, both have equal value and both are worthy of equal honor.

Is diversity consistent with equality?

Matthew 25:14-15 *The Kingdom of Heaven can be illustrated by the story of a man going on a trip. He called together his servants and gave them money to invest for him while he was gone. He gave five bags of gold to one, two bags of gold to another, and one bag of gold to the last—dividing it in proportion to their abilities—and then left on his trip.*

1 Corinthians 12:4, 6 *Now there are different kinds of spiritual gifts, but it is the same Holy Spirit who is the source of them all. . . . There are different ways God works in our lives, but it is the same God who does the work through all of us.*
Being equal is not synonymous with being identical. Diversity is a part of God's plan. In God's eyes we are not all alike; we are all equal.

121

PROMISE FROM GOD: Ephesians 2:18
Now all of us, both Jews and Gentiles, may come to the Father through the same Holy Spirit because of what Christ has done for us.

Example

What examples (role models) should we follow?

Exodus 23:24 *Do not worship the gods of these other nations . . . and never follow their evil example.*

1 Corinthians 11:1 *And you should follow my example, just as I follow Christ's.*
We can find some characteristics to follow in other people, but we are never to follow any sinful example. In Jesus Christ, we find all of the characteristics to follow. Following Jesus' example is always right.

In what ways can we be a good example to each other?

1 Thessalonians 1:5 *When we brought you the Good News, it was not only with words but also with power, for the Holy Spirit gave you full assurance that what we said was true. And you know that the way we lived among you was further proof of the truth of our message.*

A good role model is responsible and accountable.

Jeremiah 1:10 *Today I appoint you to stand up against nations and kingdoms.*
A good role model not only does what is right but also speaks out against wrong.

Hosea 6:3 *Let us press on to know him!*
Being a good role model doesn't mean that you are perfect but that you are pushing toward maturity.

Matthew 20:28 *For even I, the Son of Man, came here not to be served but to serve others.*
Being a good role model doesn't make you a celebrity; it makes you a servant.

Titus 2:7 *And you yourself must be an example to them by doing good deeds of every kind.*
A good role model does good for others.

PROMISE FROM GOD: 1 Timothy 4:12, 16 *Be an example to all believers in what you teach, in the way you live, in your love, your faith, and your purity. . . . Stay true to what is right, and God will save you and those who hear you.*

Expectations

What should we expect as we look to the future?

Proverbs 11:23 *The godly can look forward to happiness, while the wicked can expect only wrath.*

2 Corinthians 3:8 *Shouldn't we expect far greater glory when the Holy Spirit is giving life?*

Hebrews 10:26-27 *Dear friends, if we deliberately continue sinning after we have received a full knowledge of the truth, there is no other sacrifice that will cover these sins. There will be nothing to look forward to but the terrible expectation of God's judgment and the raging fire that will consume his enemies.*
If we live for God, we can expect a glorious future; if we live in rebellion against God, we can expect judgment.

Romans 5:3-5 *We can rejoice, too, when we run into problems and trials, for we know that they are good for us—they help us learn to endure. And endurance develops strength of character in us, and character strengthens our confident expectation of salvation. And this expectation will not disappoint us. For we know how dearly God loves us, because he has given us the Holy Spirit to fill our hearts with his love.*
Those who have trusted in Christ for salvation anticipate eternal life with God.

Luke 2:25 *Now there was a man named Simeon who lived in Jerusalem. He was a righteous man and very devout. He was filled with the Holy Spirit, and he eagerly expected the Messiah to come and rescue Israel.* We can live in eager expectation of Christ's coming again.

James 1:5-7 *If you need wisdom—if you want to know what God wants you to do—ask him, and he will gladly tell you. He will not resent your asking. But when you ask him, be sure that you really expect him to answer, for a doubtful mind is as unsettled as a wave of the sea that is driven and tossed by the wind. People like that should not expect to receive anything from the Lord.* When we pray, we can be confident that God will answer us.

What should we not expect?

Psalm 10:6 *They say to themselves, "Nothing bad will ever happen to us! We will be free of trouble forever!"*

Isaiah 33:1 *You expect others to respect their promises to you, while you betray your promises to them. Now you, too, will be betrayed and destroyed!*

Ezekiel 33:13 *When I tell righteous people that they will live, but then they sin, expecting their past righteousness to save them, then none of their good deeds will be remembered. I will destroy them for their sins.*

We cannot live in sin and expect to never suffer the consequences.

Ecclesiastes 10:8-9 *When you dig a well, you may fall in. When you demolish an old wall, you could be bitten by a snake. When you work in a quarry, stones might fall and crush you! When you chop wood, there is danger with each stroke of your ax! Such are the risks of life.*
We should not expect life to be free from danger and risk.

2 Corinthians 11:7 *I humbled myself and honored you by preaching God's Good News to you without expecting anything in return.*
We should not expect to be rewarded by others for serving God and obeying him.

Esther 6:6 *The king said, "What should I do to honor a man who truly pleases me?" Haman thought to himself, "Whom would the king wish to honor more than me?"*
We should not expect honor for ourselves (see Esther 6:7-12).

Luke 13:26-27 *You will say, "But we ate and drank with you, and you taught in our streets." And he will reply, "I tell you, I don't know you. Go away, all you who do evil."*
We should not expect to get into heaven by merely knowing about Christ. We must personally trust in him for forgiveness and eternal life.

Isaiah 55:8 *"My thoughts are completely different from yours," says the LORD. "And my ways are far beyond anything you could imagine."*
We should not expect God to do things our way.

PROMISE FROM GOD: 1 Peter 1:3-4
All honor to the God and Father of our Lord Jesus Christ, for it is by his boundless mercy that God has given us the privilege of being born again. Now we live with a wonderful expectation because Jesus Christ rose again from the dead. For God has reserved a priceless inheritance for his children. It is kept in heaven for you, pure and undefiled, beyond the reach of change and decay.

Failure

How do we keep from failing?

Numbers 14:22 *Not one of these people will ever enter that land. They have seen my glorious presence and the miraculous signs I performed both in Egypt and in the wilderness, but again and again they tested me by refusing to listen.*

Joshua 7:10-12 *The LORD said to Joshua, "Get up! Why are you lying on your face like this? Israel has sinned and broken my covenant! . . . That is why the Israelites are running from their enemies in defeat. For now Israel has been set apart for destruction."*

Hebrews 4:6 *God's rest is there for people to enter. But those who formerly heard the Good News failed to enter because they disobeyed God.*
Failure results when we ignore God's voice and disobey God's word. We can prevent failure by listening to God and doing what he says.

Matthew 7:24-27 *"Anyone who listens to my teaching and obeys me is wise, like a person who builds a house on solid rock. Though the rain comes in torrents and the floodwaters rise and the winds beat against that house, it won't collapse, because it is built on rock. But anyone who hears my teaching and ignores it is foolish, like a person who builds a house on sand. When the rains and floods come and the winds beat against that house, it will fall with a mighty crash."*
Listening to Christ and his instructions will help us avoid failure.

1 Chronicles 28:20 *Be strong and courageous, and do the work. Don't be afraid or discouraged by the size of the task, for the LORD God, my God, is with you. He will not fail you or forsake you. He will see to it that all the work . . . is finished correctly.*
Courage and perseverance help prevent failure, especially when we know we are in God's will.

Proverbs 15:22 *Plans go wrong for lack of advice; many counselors bring success.*
Getting good advice helps prevent failure.

Isaiah 42:23 *Will not even one of you apply these lessons from the past and see the ruin that awaits you?*
We can avoid failure by learning from the mistakes of the past.

Lamentations 3:23 *Great is his faithfulness; his mercies begin afresh each day.*
God's great faithfulness sustains us daily—he helps us avoid failure and helps us start over if we do fail.

When we have failed, how do we get past it and move on?

1 Kings 8:33-34 *If your people Israel are defeated by their enemies because they have sinned against you, and if they turn to you and call on your name and pray to you here in this Temple, then hear from heaven and forgive their sins and return them to this land you gave their ancestors.*
Turning to God in repentance and trust is the best response to our own failure.

2 Corinthians 4:9 *We are hunted down, but God never abandons us. We get knocked down, but we get up again and keep going.*
When we fail, we can get up again with the hope that faith in God brings.

Hebrews 4:15-16 *This High Priest of ours understands our weaknesses. . . . So let us come boldly to the throne of our gracious God . . . [to] find grace to help us when we need it.*

Realize that God's work is not limited by our failures. He does not reject us in our weakness but embraces us so that we can receive strength to be all he intended us to be.

PROMISE FROM GOD: Psalm 37:23-24 *The steps of the godly are directed by the LORD. He delights in every detail of their lives. Though they stumble, they will not fall, for the LORD holds them by the hand.*

Faithfulness

see **Commitment**

Family

see also **Children** *and* **Parenting**

What is family? How does the Bible define it?

Genesis 2:24 *A man leaves his father and mother and is joined to his wife, and the two are united into one.*

Psalm 127:3 *Children are a gift from the LORD; they are a reward from him.*

Ephesians 2:19 *You are members of God's family.*

James 1:18 *In his goodness he chose to make us his own children.*
The Bible talks about both an earthly family—made up of husband, wife, and children—and the family of God, made up of believers united together by the bond of faith.

1 Chronicles 9:1 *All Israel was listed in the genealogical record in The Book of the Kings of Israel.*
The Bible lists many genealogies, showing the family as central and fundamental to the development of people and of nations.

Joshua 24:15 *But as for me and my family, we will serve the LORD.*

Proverbs 6:20 *My son, obey your father's commands, and don't neglect your mother's teaching.*
God intended families to be united in serving him. The family is one of God's greatest resources for communicating truth and effecting change in any community.

What is my responsibility to my family?

Deuteronomy 6:6-7 *You must commit yourselves wholeheartedly to these commands I am giving you today. Repeat them again and again to your children. Talk about them when you are at home.*

Proverbs 22:6 *Teach your children to choose the right path, and when they are older, they will remain upon it.*
As a parent, you are responsible for the moral and spiritual training of your children. Explain the Good News of Jesus to them!

2 Timothy 1:5 *I know that you sincerely trust the Lord, for you have the faith of your mother, Eunice, and your grandmother, Lois.*

Exodus 10:2 *You will be able to tell wonderful stories to your children and grandchildren about the marvelous things I am doing . . . to prove that I am the LORD.*
As a parent, you have the responsibility and the privilege of sharing your faith with your children. Tell them what God has done in your life!

Ephesians 6:4 *Now a word to you fathers. Don't make your children angry by the way you treat them. Rather, bring them up with the discipline and instruction approved by the Lord.*
A father has the responsibility of disciplining and instructing his children, and doing so with consistency, integrity, and love. Inconsistency, harshness, and hypocrisy are surefire ways to make your children angry.

Titus 2:4-5 *These older women must train the younger women to love their husbands and their children, to live wisely and be pure, to take care of their homes, to do good.*

Proverbs 31:27 *She carefully watches all that goes on in her household and does not have to bear the consequences of laziness.*
A wife and mother has the responsibility of loving her husband and children.

PROMISE FROM GOD: Psalm 102:28 *The children of your people will live in security. Their children's children will thrive in your presence.*

Faults

How should we confront our own faults?

Romans 7:18-19 *I know I am rotten through and through so far as my old sinful nature is concerned. No matter which way I turn, I can't make myself do right. I want to, but I can't. When I want to do good, I don't. And when I try not to do wrong, I do it anyway.*

Galatians 5:17 *The old sinful nature loves to do evil, which is just opposite from what the Holy Spirit wants. And the Spirit gives us desires that are opposite from what the sinful nature desires. These two forces are constantly fighting each other, and your choices are never free from this conflict.*
We must recognize our sin as the root of our faults and our problems.

Psalm 44:21 *God would surely have known it, for he knows the secrets of every heart.*

Psalm 90:8 *You spread out our sins before you—our secret sins—and you see them all.*

Ecclesiastes 12:14 *God will judge us for everything we do, including every secret thing, whether good or bad.*
We should be quick to recognize and admit our faults to God. We must believe that God knows our every fault; we cannot hide our faults from him.

Mark 6:18 *John kept telling Herod, "It is illegal for you to marry your brother's wife."*

Acts 5:3 *Then Peter said, "Ananias, why has Satan filled your heart? You lied to the Holy Spirit, and you kept some of the money for yourself."*
We must be open to accept godly criticism from others.

Psalm 51:3-4 *For I recognize my shameful deeds—they haunt me day and night. Against you, and you alone, have I sinned; I have done what is evil in your sight. You will be proved right in what you say, and your judgment against me is just.*

Jonah 1:12 *"Throw me into the sea," Jonah said, "and it will become calm again. For I know that this terrible storm is all my fault."*

Luke 15:18 *I will go home to my father and say, "Father, I have sinned against both heaven and you."* We are to accept the responsibility for and the consequences of our own faults.

How should I keep from focusing on others' faults?

Galatians 6:5 *We are each responsible for our own conduct.*

Matthew 7:1, 3, 5 *Stop judging others, and you will not be judged. . . . Why worry about a speck in your friend's eye when you have a log in your own? . . . First get rid of the log from your own eye; then perhaps you will see well enough to deal with the speck in your friend's eye.*

James 4:11-12 *Don't speak evil against each other, my dear brothers and sisters . . . you are not a judge who can decide whether the law is right or wrong. Your job is to obey it. God alone, who made the law, can rightly judge among us . . . what right do you have to condemn your neighbor?*
We must deal with our own faults and let God be the judge of others. We should see ourselves as God sees us and be humbled. There are times when we must point out others' faults (Prov. 27:6), but our focus should not be judgmental. Instead it must be loving and corrective.

Galatians 6:1 *Dear friends, if a Christian is overcome by some sin, you who are godly should gently and humbly help that person back onto the right path.*

Ephesians 4:2 *Be humble and gentle. Be patient with each other, making allowance for each other's faults because of your love.*
When dealing with others' faults, our focus must be to help them not to hurt them. We must always be humble, gentle, and patient with others.

PROMISES FROM GOD: 1 Peter 4:8 *Love covers a multitude of sins.*

Colossians 1:22 *Now he has brought you back as his friends. He has done this through his death on the cross in his own human body. As a result, he has brought you into the very presence of God, and you are holy and blameless as you stand before him without a single fault.*

Feelings

How should we respond to our feelings?

Psalm 102:1-2 *LORD, hear my prayer! Listen to my plea! Don't turn away from me in my time of distress. Bend down your ear and answer me quickly when I call to you.*

Job 7:11 *I cannot keep from speaking. I must express my anguish. I must complain in my bitterness.*

Psalm 62:8 *O my people, trust in him at all times. Pour out your heart to him, for God is our refuge.*
We should honestly tell God our feelings. Pouring out your heart to him can be an act of faith and devotion.

Psalm 43:5 *Why am I discouraged? Why so sad? I will put my hope in God! I will praise him again—my Savior and my God!*
We can respond to feelings of discouragement and sadness by turning to God in faith. He gives hope for the future.

How should we control our feelings?

Proverbs 4:23 *Above all else, guard your heart, for it affects everything you do.*
We must guard our minds and hearts. Being aware of the huge impact our emotions have on our lives can prevent us from exposing ourselves to things that might subvert our emotions.

2 Peter 1:6 *Knowing God leads to self-control. Self-control leads to patient endurance, and patient endurance leads to godliness.*

Colossians 3:8, 10 *Now is the time to get rid of anger, rage. . . . You have clothed yourselves with a brand-new nature that is continually being renewed as you learn more and more about Christ, who created this new nature within you.*

Knowing God and following Christ transform our lives. God gives us the self-control to avoid those emotions that might lead us impulsively into sin.

Ephesians 4:23 *There must be a spiritual renewal of your thoughts and attitudes.*

Romans 13:14 *Let the Lord Jesus Christ take control of you, and don't think of ways to indulge your evil desires.*

Galatians 5:22-23 *When the Holy Spirit controls our lives, he will produce this kind of fruit in us: love, joy, peace, patience, kindness, goodness, faithfulness, gentleness, and self-control. Here there is no conflict with the law.*

We must ask the Lord to take control of us by his Holy Spirit. When his Spirit lives within us, he keeps our emotions pure. The emotions which come from the Holy Spirit are much more exciting, joyful, and satisfying than the emotions that come from our sinful nature.

What are some of the dangers of feelings?

Ephesians 4:26 *Don't sin by letting anger gain control over you.*

Our feelings can lead us into sin.

Numbers 14:1-3 *Then all the people began weeping aloud, and they cried all night. Their voices rose in a great chorus of complaint against Moses and Aaron. "We wish we had died in Egypt, or even here in the wilderness!" they wailed. "Why is the LORD taking us to this country only to have us die in battle?"*
Our feelings can cause us to forget the truth about God.

Amos 6:1 *How terrible it will be for you who lounge in luxury and think you are secure in Jerusalem and Samaria!*
Our feelings can give us a false sense of security.

Galatians 5:16-17 *I advise you to live according to your new life in the Holy Spirit. Then you won't be doing what your sinful nature craves. The old sinful nature loves to do evil, which is just opposite from what the Holy Spirit wants.*
Our feelings are not a reliable guide, because they can be influenced by both our sinful nature and by the Holy Spirit. The best way to know what the Holy Spirit wants is not from our feelings but from the words of Scripture.

Song of Songs 2:7 *Promise me, O women of Jerusalem, by the swift gazelles and the deer of the wild, not to awaken love until the time is right.*
An impatient response to our feelings can cause us to forfeit God's perfect timing for us.

PROMISE FROM GOD: Psalm 28:7
The LORD is my strength, my shield from every danger. I trust in him with all my heart. He helps me, and my heart is filled with joy. I burst out in songs of thanksgiving.

Flexibility

How can we be more flexible in our relationships?

James 3:17 *But the wisdom that comes from heaven is first of all pure. It is also peace loving, gentle at all times, and willing to yield to others. It is full of mercy and good deeds. It shows no partiality and is always sincere.*
With the wisdom that God gives, we can see others through God's eyes. This prevents us from judging people by our own standards.

Genesis 13:9 *"Take your choice of any section of the land you want, and we will separate. If you want that area over there, then I'll stay here. If you want to stay in this area, then I'll move on to another place."*
We can give up something we want in order to have a better relationship with others.

1 Kings 3:26 *Then the woman who really was the mother of the living child, and who loved him very much, cried out, "Oh no, my lord! Give her the*

child—please do not kill him!" But the other woman said, "All right, he will be neither yours nor mine; divide him between us!"

We can give up something we want for the sake of another.

How can we be more flexible in responding to God?

Matthew 26:42 *"My Father! If this cup cannot be taken away until I drink it, your will be done."*
We can tell God our Father what we want, but we must always be willing to do as he pleases.

Isaiah 6:8 *Then I heard the Lord asking, "Whom should I send as a messenger to my people? Who will go for us?" And I said, "Lord, I'll go! Send me."*

Luke 1:38 *Mary responded, "I am the Lord's servant, and I am willing to accept whatever he wants. May everything you have said come true." And then the angel left.*
We must listen for and willingly respond to God's direction for our lives.

PROMISE FROM GOD: James 3:17
The wisdom that comes from heaven is first of all pure. It is also peace loving, gentle at all times, and willing to yield to others. It is full of mercy and good deeds. It shows no partiality and is always sincere.

Forgiveness

What does it really mean to be forgiven?

Colossians 1:22 *You are holy and blameless as you stand before him without a single fault.*

Isaiah 1:18 *No matter how deep the stain of your sins, I can remove it. I can make you as clean as freshly fallen snow.*
Forgiveness means that God looks at us as though we have never sinned. When we receive his forgiveness, we are blameless before him.

Acts 8:22-23 *Turn from your wickedness and pray to the Lord. Perhaps he will forgive your evil thoughts, for I can see that you are full of bitterness and held captive by sin.*
God forgives us even when we are in slavery to sin.

Romans 4:7 *Oh, what joy for those whose disobedience is forgiven, whose sins are put out of sight.*
Forgiveness brings great joy.

How do I experience forgiveness when I have done wrong?

Matthew 26:28 *This is my blood, which seals the covenant between God and his people. It is poured out to forgive the sins of many.*

Jesus died so that God's forgiveness would be freely available to us.

Psalm 51:4 *Against you, and you alone, have I sinned; I have done what is evil in your sight.*
We must realize that we wrong God with our sin.

2 Chronicles 7:14 *If my people who are called by my name will humble themselves and pray and seek my face and turn from their wicked ways, I will hear from heaven and will forgive their sins and heal their land.*

1 John 1:8-9 *If we say we have no sin, we are only fooling ourselves and refusing to accept the truth. But if we confess our sins to him, he is faithful and just to forgive us and to cleanse us from every wrong.*
We will receive God's forgiveness when we confess our sins to him, stop doing what is wrong, and turn to him with our heart.

Acts 10:43 *Everyone who believes in him will have their sins forgiven through his name.*

Acts 13:38 *In this man Jesus there is forgiveness for your sins.*
We receive God's forgiveness by trusting in Christ.

How should we forgive others who hurt us?

Matthew 5:44 *Love your enemies! Pray for those who persecute you!*

143

Forgiveness means praying for those who hate us and hurt us.

Matthew 6:14-15 *If you forgive those who sin against you, your heavenly Father will forgive you. But if you refuse to forgive others, your Father will not forgive your sins.*
We must not refuse to forgive others. If we do so we won't understand or experience God's forgiveness.

Matthew 18:21-22 *Peter came to him and asked, "Lord, how often should I forgive someone who sins against me? Seven times?" "No!" Jesus replied, "seventy times seven!"*
Just as God forgives us without limit, we should forgive others without counting how many times.

1 Peter 3:8-9 *Don't repay evil for evil. Don't retaliate when people say unkind things about you. Instead, pay them back with a blessing. That is what God wants you to do, and he will bless you for it.*
When people say hurtful things about us, God wants us to respond by blessing them.

PROMISES FROM GOD: Isaiah 1:18 *No matter how deep the stain of your sins, I can remove it. I can make you as clean as freshly fallen snow.*

1 John 1:9 *But if we confess our sins to him, he is faithful and just to forgive us and to cleanse us from every wrong.*

Friendship

What is the mark of true friendship?

Proverbs 17:17 *A friend is always loyal, and a brother is born to help in time of need.*

1 Samuel 18:3 *Jonathan made a special vow to be David's friend.*
Some friendships are fleeting, and some are lasting. True friendships are glued together with bonds of loyalty and commitment. They remain intact despite changing external circumstances.

What gets in the way of friendships?

1 Samuel 18:8-9 *"What's this?" [Saul] said. "They credit David with ten thousands and me with only thousands. Next they'll be making him their king!" So from that time on Saul kept a jealous eye on David.*
Jealousy is the great dividing force of friendships. Envy will soon turn to anger and bitterness, causing you to separate yourself from the one you truly cared for.

Psalm 41:9 *Even my best friend, the one I trusted completely . . . has turned against me.*
When respect or trust is seriously damaged, even the closest friendship is at risk.

Does the Bible offer any guidelines for friendships?

1 Corinthians 13:4-5 *Love is patient and kind. Love is not jealous or boastful or proud or rude. Love does not demand its own way.*
Paul's timeless description of Christian love is the standard of respect and decency that should mark all of our relationships.

PROMISE FROM GOD: Leviticus 26:12 *I will walk among you; I will be your God, and you will be my people.*

Fun

see Happiness

Future

What can we do in our relationships today to positively impact our future?

Esther 9:28 *These days would be remembered and kept from generation to generation and celebrated by every family throughout the provinces and cities of the empire. These days would never cease to be celebrated among the Jews, nor would the memory of what happened ever die out among their descendants.*

Psalm 78:4 *We will not hide these truths from our children but will tell the next generation about the glorious deeds of the LORD. We will tell of his power and the mighty miracles he did.*

Celebrating and sharing the Lord with our spouse, our family, and our friends are investments in the future. Traditions affirm the past, help us delight in the present, and secure the future.

PROMISES FROM GOD:

1 Corinthians 2:9 *That is what the Scriptures mean when they say, "No eye has seen, no ear has heard, and no mind has imagined what God has prepared for those who love him."*

Jeremiah 29:11 *"For I know the plans I have for you," says the Lord. "They are plans for good and not for disaster, to give you a future and a hope."*

Gifts

What are some gifts we can give to each other?

1 Corinthians 13:4-7 *Love is patient and kind. Love is not jealous or boastful or proud or rude. Love does not demand its own way. Love is not irritable, and it keeps no record of when it has been wronged. It is never glad about injustice but rejoices*

whenever the truth wins out. Love never gives up, never loses faith, is always hopeful, and endures through every circumstance.
We can give one another the gift of love.

Matthew 6:14 *If you forgive those who sin against you, your heavenly Father will forgive you.*
We can give each other the gift of forgiveness. This merely reflects God's greater gift of forgiveness to us.

1 Peter 3:7 *In the same way, you husbands must give honor to your wives. Treat her with understanding as you live together.*

Proverbs 31:28-29 *Her children stand and bless her. Her husband praises her: "There are many virtuous and capable women in the world, but you surpass them all!"*
We can give our spouses honor and respect. Isn't that the gift we appreciate from them?

Romans 1:11-12 *For I long to visit you so I can share a spiritual blessing with you that will help you grow strong in the Lord. I'm eager to encourage you in your faith, but I also want to be encouraged by yours. In this way, each of us will be a blessing to the other.*
We can spiritually bless one another by encouraging each other to grow stronger in the Lord.

What are some of the results of giving gifts?

2 Corinthians 9:11-14 *Yes, you will be enriched so that you can give even more generously. And when we take your gifts to those who need them, they will break out in thanksgiving to God. So two good things will happen—the needs of the Christians in Jerusalem will be met, and they will joyfully express their thanksgiving to God. You will be glorifying God through your generous gifts.*

Giving gifts glorifies God and enriches our own lives. Others will thank God and honor him as their needs are met.

1 Peter 4:10 *God has given gifts to each of you from his great variety of spiritual gifts. Manage them well so that God's generosity can flow through you.*

2 Corinthians 9:10 *For God is the one who gives seed to the farmer and then bread to eat. In the same way, he will give you many opportunities to do good, and he will produce a great harvest of generosity in you.*

The giver and the receiver both experience God's generosity.

Ecclesiastes 11:1 *Give generously, for your gifts will return to you later.*

Luke 6:38 *If you give, you will receive. Your gift will return to you in full measure, pressed down, shaken together to make room for more, and running over.*

Those who give receive God's blessing. Giving does not drain us; it fills us.

How should we receive gifts from others?

Luke 17:12-13, 15-16 *As he entered a village there, ten lepers stood at a distance, crying out, "Jesus, Master, have mercy on us!" . . . One of them, when he saw that he was healed, came back to Jesus, shouting, "Praise God, I'm healed!" He fell face down on the ground at Jesus' feet, thanking him for what he had done.*
When we receive gifts, we should express our sincere thanks.

Matthew 25:20-21 *The servant to whom he had entrusted the five bags of gold said, "Sir, you gave me five bags of gold to invest, and I have doubled the amount." The master was full of praise. "Well done, my good and faithful servant. You have been faithful in handling this small amount, so now I will give you many more responsibilities."*

2 Timothy 1:6 *Fan into flames the spiritual gift God gave you.*

1 Peter 4:10 *God has given gifts to each of you from his great variety of spiritual gifts. Manage them well so that God's generosity can flow through you.*
When we receive a gift, we should faithfully and gratefully use it as fully as possible.

PROMISE FROM GOD: Psalm 84:11
For the LORD God is our light and protector. He gives us grace and glory. No good thing will the LORD withhold from those who do what is right.

Happiness

Does God promise us happiness?

Philippians 4:4, 12 *Always be full of joy in the Lord. I say it again—rejoice! . . . I have learned the secret of living in every situation.*

James 1:2 *Whenever trouble comes your way, let it be an opportunity for joy.*
The Bible assumes problems will come our way, but God promises lasting joy for all those who believe in him. His joy stays with us despite our problems.

Where do we get real, lasting happiness?

Hebrews 12:1-2 *Let us run with endurance the race that God has set before us . . . by keeping our eyes on Jesus. . . . He was willing to die a shameful death on the cross because of the joy he knew would be his afterward.*
Keep your eyes on Jesus and follow his example of pressing on toward a joyful future.

Psalm 112:1 *Happy are those who fear the LORD. Yes, happy are those who delight in doing what he commands.*
God promises true happiness to those who revere him, trust him, and do what he commands.

Psalm 16:8-9 *I know the LORD is always with me. . . . No wonder my heart is filled with joy.*
Happiness is based on God's presence within us, which brings true contentment.

Galatians 5:22 *But when the Holy Spirit controls our lives, he will produce this kind of fruit in us: love, joy, peace.*
The presence of the Holy Spirit in our lives produces joy.

Psalm 119:2 *Happy are those who obey his decrees and search for him with all their hearts.*

Philippians 1:25 *I will continue with you so that you will grow and experience the joy of your faith.*
Devotion, faith, and obedience to God bring happiness. God has promised that when we truly seek him, we will surely find him (Jer. 29:13-14).

Matthew 25:21 *You have been faithful in handling this small amount. . . . Let's celebrate together!*
A job well done is an occasion for joy.

How can we bring happiness to others?

Romans 12:10 *Love each other with genuine affection, and take delight in honoring each other.*
Treating others with God's love will bring them happiness.

2 Corinthians 7:13 *In addition to our own encouragement, we were especially delighted to see how happy Titus was at the way you welcomed him and set his mind at ease.*
Exercising hospitality toward others will help them relax and be happy.

PROMISE FROM GOD: Proverbs 11:23 *The godly can look forward to happiness, while the wicked can expect only wrath.*

Heart

How do I guard and protect my heart?

Proverbs 4:23 *Above all else, guard your heart, for it affects everything you do.*

1 John 5:21 *Dear children, keep away from anything that might take God's place in your hearts.*

Ephesians 3:17 *And I pray that Christ will be more and more at home in your hearts as you trust in him. May your roots go down deep into the soil of God's marvelous love.*

Keeping God at the center of your heart prevents anything else from taking that place.

How do I recover from a broken heart?

Psalm 61:2 *From the ends of the earth, I will cry to you for help, for my heart is overwhelmed. Lead me to the towering rock of safety.*
Pouring your heart out in prayer to God can help mend your broken heart.

PROMISE FROM GOD: Ezekiel 36:26 *And I will give you a new heart with new and right desires, and I will put a new spirit in you. I will take out your stony heart of sin and give you a new, obedient heart.*

Home

How can we experience God's blessing on our home?

Psalm 127:1 *Unless the LORD builds a house, the work of the builders is useless.*
God desires an active role in our homes. He offers to be not only the architect but the builder.

Proverbs 3:33 *The curse of the LORD is on the house of the wicked, but his blessing is on the home of the upright.*

Proverbs 12:7 *The wicked perish and are gone, but the children of the godly stand firm.*
God's blessing is promised to those who are righteous.

1 Chronicles 13:14 *The Ark of God remained there with the family of Obed-edom for three months, and the LORD blessed him and his entire household.*
God's blessing comes to a home where he is present.

What makes a godly home?

Colossians 3:14 *And the most important piece of clothing you must wear is love. Love is what binds us all together in perfect harmony.*

Ephesians 5:28 *Husbands ought to love their wives as they love their own bodies.*
Love makes a home godly.

Colossians 3:13 *You must make allowance for each other's faults and forgive the person who offends you. Remember, the Lord forgave you, so you must forgive others.*
Forgiving one another helps our homes reflect God's character.

Proverbs 23:24 *The father of godly children has cause for joy. What a pleasure it is to have wise children.*

Proverbs 27:11 *My child, how happy I will be if you turn out to be wise! Then I will be able to answer my critics.*

Wisdom brings godly joy to a home.

1 Peter 3:7 *In the same way, you husbands must give honor to your wives. Treat her with understanding as you live together. She may be weaker than you are, but she is your equal partner in God's gift of new life. If you don't treat her as you should, your prayers will not be heard.*

Ephesians 6:2 *"Honor your father and mother." This is the first of the Ten Commandments that ends with a promise.*
Treating one another with honor gives our homes a godly character.

Ephesians 5:22-24 *You wives will submit to your husbands as you do to the Lord. For a husband is the head of his wife as Christ is the head of his body, the church; he gave his life to be her Savior. As the church submits to Christ, so you wives must submit to your husbands in everything.*

Ephesians 6:1 *Children, obey your parents because you belong to the Lord, for this is the right thing to do.*
Submission to God's authority in the home is an act of godliness.

Proverbs 19:18 *Discipline your children while there is hope. If you don't, you will ruin their lives.*
Discipline builds godly character in our children.

PROMISE FROM GOD: Proverbs 14:11
The house of the wicked will perish, but the tent of the godly will flourish.

Honesty

see **Integrity**

Honor

see **Respect**

Hospitality

To whom are we to be hospitable?

Romans 12:13 *When God's children are in need, be the one to help them out. And get into the habit of inviting guests home for dinner or, if they need lodging, for the night.*
We should be hospitable to other Christians.

3 John 1:5 *Dear friend, you are doing a good work for God when you take care of the traveling teachers who are passing through, even though they are strangers to you.*
We should be hospitable to those who are working for God in ministry.

Hebrews 13:2 *Don't forget to show hospitality to strangers, for some who have done this have entertained angels without realizing it!*
We should be hospitable to strangers when the opportunity arises.

Isaiah 58:7 *I want you to share your food with the hungry and to welcome poor wanderers into your homes. Give clothes to those who need them, and do not hide from relatives who need your help.*
We should give to the hungry, poor, and needy—whoever they may be.

Luke 14:12-14 *"When you put on a luncheon or a dinner," he said, "don't invite your friends, brothers, relatives, and rich neighbors. For they will repay you by inviting you back. Instead, invite the poor, the crippled, the lame, and the blind. Then at the resurrection of the godly, God will reward you for inviting those who could not repay you."*
We should seek to bless those who cannot repay us.

How can we make our homes places of hospitality?

2 Kings 4:8 *One day Elisha went to the town of Shunem. A wealthy woman lived there, and she invited him to eat some food. From then on, whenever he passed that way, he would stop there to eat.*

Philemon 1:22 *Please keep a guest room ready for me, for I am hoping that God will answer your prayers and let me return to you soon.*
We can host others in our home.

Genesis 29:13 *As soon as Laban heard about Jacob's arrival, he rushed out to meet him and greeted him warmly. Laban then brought him home.*
We can give others a warm welcome to our home.

Judges 19:18-21 *"You are welcome to stay with me," the old man said. "I will give you anything you might need. But whatever you do, don't spend the night in the square." So he took them home with him and fed their donkeys. After they washed their feet, they had supper together.*
We can be sensitive to the needs of our guests.

PROMISE FROM GOD:
Matthew 25:35-36, 40 *I was hungry, and you fed me. I was thirsty, and you gave me a drink. . . . I was sick, and you cared for me. . . . I assure you, when you did it to one of the least of these my brothers and sisters, you were doing it to me!*

Humility

see also Ego

What is true humility?

Zephaniah 3:12 *Those who are left will be the lowly and the humble, for it is they who trust in the name of the LORD.*
Humility is not thinking too highly of yourself.

Titus 3:2 *They must not speak evil of anyone, and they must avoid quarreling. Instead, they should be gentle and show true humility to everyone.*
Humility is gentleness.

Psalm 51:3-4 *For I recognize my shameful deeds—they haunt me day and night. Against you, and you alone, have I sinned; I have done what is evil in your sight. You will be proved right in what you say, and your judgment against me is just.*
Humility is willingness to confess sin.

How do we become humble?

Deuteronomy 8:2-3 *Remember how the LORD your God led you through the wilderness for forty years, humbling you and testing you to prove your character, and to find out whether or not you would really obey his commands. Yes, he humbled you by*

letting you go hungry and then feeding you with manna. . . . He did it to teach you that people need more than bread for their life.
Humility comes when we recognize that we need God.

Philippians 2:3 *Don't be selfish; don't live to make a good impression on others. Be humble, thinking of others as better than yourself.*
Humility means not thinking of yourself more highly than others.

How will humility change our relationships with others?

Ephesians 4:2 *Be humble and gentle. Be patient with each other, making allowance for each other's faults because of your love.*

Matthew 7:3 *Why worry about a speck in your friend's eye when you have a log in your own?*
Loving humility overlooks the faults of others in light of our own.

PROMISE FROM GOD: Psalm 18:27 *You rescue those who are humble, but you humiliate the proud.*

Husbands

What are some ways I can love my husband?

1 Peter 3:5 *That is the way the holy women of old made themselves beautiful. They trusted God and accepted the authority of their husbands.*
You can accept your husband's authority.

Proverbs 12:4 *A worthy wife is her husband's joy and crown; a shameful wife saps his strength.*
You can give him joy.

Proverbs 31:11 *Her husband can trust her, and she will greatly enrich his life.*
You can be trustworthy.

1 Corinthians 7:34 *The married woman must be concerned about her earthly responsibilities and how to please her husband.*
I can think of ways to please him.

How can I best help my husband if he does not know Jesus Christ as his Savior and Lord?

1 Corinthians 7:13-16 *And if a Christian woman has a husband who is an unbeliever, and he is willing to continue living with her, she must not leave him. For the Christian wife brings holiness to her marriage, and the Christian husband brings holiness*

162

to his marriage. Otherwise, your children would not have a godly influence, but now they are set apart for him. . . . You wives must remember that your husbands might be converted because of you. And you husbands must remember that your wives might be converted because of you.

1 Peter 3:1 *In the same way, you wives must accept the authority of your husbands, even those who refuse to accept the Good News. Your godly lives will speak to them better than any words. They will be won over.*
Godly loving is the best way to witness to an unbelieving mate.

How should a husband treat his wife?

Ephesians 5:25 *And you husbands must love your wives with the same love Christ showed the church. He gave up his life for her.*
Husbands should love their wives sacrificially with the depth of love that Christ showed when he died for us.

Proverbs 31:28-29 *Her children stand and bless her. Her husband praises her: "There are many virtuous and capable women in the world, but you surpass them all!"*
Husbands should admire their wives and praise them openly.

Colossians 3:19 *And you husbands must love your wives and never treat them harshly.*
Husbands should love their wives with kindness and gentleness.

PROMISE FROM GOD: Proverbs 31:11 *Her husband can trust her, and she will greatly enrich his life.*

Immorality

How does immorality affect our relationships?

Hebrews 13:4 *Give honor to marriage, and remain faithful to one another in marriage. God will surely judge people who are immoral and those who commit adultery.*

Matthew 5:32 *But I say that a man who divorces his wife, unless she has been unfaithful, causes her to commit adultery. And anyone who marries a divorced woman commits adultery.*
Immorality can destroy marriage and family relationships.

How can we avoid falling into immorality?

Judges 3:5-7 *So Israel lived among the Canaanites, Hittites, Amorites, Perizzites, Hivites, and Jebusites, and they intermarried with them. . . .*

They forgot about the LORD their God, and they worshiped the images of Baal and the Asherah poles.

Romans 6:12 *Do not let sin control the way you live; do not give in to its lustful desires.*
We are to realize the subtlety of immorality and not let sin control our lives.

1 Corinthians 7:2 *But because there is so much sexual immorality, each man should have his own wife, and each woman should have her own husband.*
Marriage can be a help in avoiding immorality because it brings greater accountability into our lives. It redirects our thoughts from lustful passion to loving passion.

Numbers 25:1-3 *While the Israelites were camped at Acacia, some of the men defiled themselves by sleeping with the local Moabite women. These women invited them to attend sacrifices to their gods, and soon the Israelites were feasting with them and worshiping the gods of Moab. Before long Israel was joining in the worship of Baal of Peor, causing the LORD's anger to blaze against his people.*

2 Timothy 2:22 *Run from anything that stimulates youthful lust. Follow anything that makes you want to do right. Pursue faith and love and peace, and enjoy the companionship of those who call on the Lord with pure hearts.*

We are to be careful of the company we keep. The more time spent with immoral company, the greater the chances of acting immorally.

How do we recover from an immoral lifestyle?

Galatians 5:19 *When you follow the desires of your sinful nature, your lives will produce these evil results: sexual immorality, impure thoughts, eagerness for lustful pleasure.*

1 Corinthians 6:18 *Run away from sexual sin! No other sin so clearly affects the body as this one does. For sexual immorality is a sin against your own body.*
We are to recognize all immorality as sin.

1 John 1:9 *But if we confess our sins to him, he is faithful and just to forgive us and to cleanse us from every wrong.*

Psalm 51:1-4 *Have mercy on me, O God, because of your unfailing love. Because of your great compassion, blot out the stain of my sins. Wash me clean from my guilt. Purify me from my sin. For I recognize my shameful deeds—they haunt me day and night. Against you, and you alone, have I sinned; I have done what is evil in your sight.*
We are to confess our sin to God.

Luke 7:37-38, 47 *A certain immoral woman heard he was there and brought a beautiful jar filled with expensive perfume. Then she knelt behind him at his feet, weeping. Her tears fell on his feet, and she wiped them off with her hair. Then she kept kissing his feet and putting perfume on them. . . . "I tell you, her sins—and they are many—have been forgiven, so she has shown me much love. But a person who is forgiven little shows only little love."*
We are to receive Christ's forgiveness.

1 Thessalonians 4:3-7 *God wants you to be holy, so you should keep clear of all sexual sin. Then each of you will control your body and live in holiness and honor—not in lustful passion as the pagans do, in their ignorance of God and his ways. Never cheat a Christian brother in this matter by taking his wife, for the Lord avenges all such sins, as we have solemnly warned you before. God has called us to be holy, not to live impure lives.*

Ephesians 4:19-24 *There must be a spiritual renewal of your thoughts and attitudes. You must display a new nature because you are a new person, created in God's likeness—righteous, holy, and true.*
True repentance should be evident in our future life choices.

PROMISE FROM GOD: Proverbs 6:23-24 *For these commands and this teaching are a lamp to light the way ahead of you. The correction of* *discipline is the way to life. These commands and this teaching will keep you from the immoral woman, from the smooth tongue of an adulterous woman.*

Infertility

How does God show his compassion on the childless?

Judges 13:3 *The angel of the LORD appeared to Manoah's wife and said, "Even though you have been unable to have children, you will soon become pregnant and give birth to a son."*

Luke 1:25 *"How kind the Lord is!" she exclaimed. "He has taken away my disgrace of having no children!"*

Genesis 30:22 *Then God remembered Rachel's plight and answered her prayers by giving her a child.*

Genesis 16:11 *And the angel also said, "You are now pregnant and will give birth to a son. You are to name him Ishmael, for the LORD has heard about your misery."*

God has the compassion and ability to give children to those who are childless. Although we do not understand why he chooses to do this for some and not for others, we can trust that he is a loving, attentive heavenly Father to us all.

Psalm 113:9 *He gives the barren woman a home, so that she becomes a happy mother. Praise the LORD!*

God gives special attention and compassion to the childless who long for children.

How can we have an attitude of hope if we are childless?

Ruth 4:13 *So Boaz married Ruth and took her home to live with him. When he slept with her, the LORD enabled her to become pregnant, and she gave birth to a son.*

Psalm 62:1, 5, 8 *I wait quietly before God, for my salvation comes from him. . . . I wait quietly before God, for my hope is in him. . . . O my people, trust in him at all times. Pour out your heart to him, for God is our refuge.*

Our hope and trust must be in God, the Creator of life. He wants us to honestly pour our hearts out to him to seek what is best from him. He is a refuge for us in our time of pain, suffering, loss, and sorrow.

How can we help others who are childless?

Genesis 25:21 *Isaac pleaded with the LORD to give Rebekah a child because she was childless. So the LORD answered Isaac's prayer, and his wife became pregnant with twins.*

We can pray to God on their behalf.

Job 24:20-21 *Wicked people are broken like a tree in the storm. For they have taken advantage of the childless who have no protecting sons. They refuse to help the needy widows.*

We can look for ways to be of practical assistance to families without children, especially as the husband and wife age. Sometimes childless parents find great joy in helping children of neighbors and friends.

PROMISE FROM GOD: Psalm 62:1,5,8 *I wait quietly before God, for my salvation comes from him. . . . I wait quietly before God, for my hope is in him. . . . O my people, trust in him at all times. Pour out your heart to him, for God is our refuge.*

Insecurity

How can feelings of insecurity affect our relationships?

Mark 9:34 *They had been arguing about which of them was the greatest.*

Feelings of insecurity can lead to discontent, arguing, and broken fellowship.

1 Samuel 18:7-9 *This was their song: "Saul has killed his thousands, and David his ten thousands!" This made Saul very angry. "What's this?" he said. "They credit David with ten thousands and me with*

only thousands. Next they'll be making him their king!" So from that time on Saul kept a jealous eye on David.

1 Samuel 18:28-29 *When the king realized how much the LORD was with David and how much Michal loved him, he became even more afraid of him, and he remained David's enemy for the rest of his life.*

Our own insecurity can result in envying another to the point of strife.

How should we deal with our feelings of insecurity?

Matthew 6:32-34 *Your heavenly Father already knows all your needs, and he will give you all you need from day to day if you live for him and make the Kingdom of God your primary concern. So don't worry about tomorrow, for tomorrow will bring its own worries. Today's trouble is enough for today.*

Realizing that God knows all of our needs and will provide for our well-being helps us feel secure.

Philippians 4:6-7 *Don't worry about anything; instead, pray about everything. Tell God what you need, and thank him for all he has done. If you do this, you will experience God's peace, which is far more wonderful than the human mind can understand.*

We are to bring our concerns to God in prayer with thanksgiving.

Ephesians 3:16-17 *I pray that from his glorious, unlimited resources he will give you mighty inner strength through his Holy Spirit. And I pray that Christ will be more and more at home in your hearts as you trust in him.*

Philippians 4:13 *For I can do everything with the help of Christ who gives me the strength I need.*
We are to rely on God's power and provision.

Psalm 37:3-5 *Trust in the LORD and do good. Then you will live safely in the land and prosper. Take delight in the LORD, and he will give you your heart's desires. Commit everything you do to the LORD. Trust him, and he will help you.*
We are to depend on God's promises.

PROMISE FROM GOD: Isaiah 26:3 *You will keep in perfect peace all who trust in you, whose thoughts are fixed on you!*

Insults

How are we to respond to insults?

Acts 18:6 *But when the Jews opposed him and insulted him, Paul shook the dust from his robe and said, "Your blood be upon your own heads—I am innocent. From now on I will go to the Gentiles."*

Proverbs 12:16 *A fool is quick-tempered, but a wise person stays calm when insulted.*

Proverbs 15:1 *A gentle answer turns away wrath, but harsh words stir up anger.*

1 Peter 3:9 *Don't repay evil for evil. Don't retaliate when people say unkind things about you. Instead, pay them back with a blessing. That is what God wants you to do, and he will bless you for it.* Sometimes it is best to ignore insults, and other times we must respond. When we do respond to insults, we should do so in a deliberate, controlled, and loving manner. All of our responses should be bathed in prayer, as we trust in God for the right words.

Matthew 5:11-12 *God blesses you when you are mocked and persecuted and lied about because you are my followers. Be happy about it! Be very glad! For a great reward awaits you in heaven. And remember, the ancient prophets were persecuted, too.*

Acts 5:41 *The apostles left the high council rejoicing that God had counted them worthy to suffer dishonor for the name of Jesus.*

1 Peter 4:14 *Be happy if you are insulted for being a Christian, for then the glorious Spirit of God will come upon you.*

Keep an eternal perspective regarding insults. We can rejoice when we are insulted for Jesus' sake because we know that in the end we will be victorious in him.

Lamentations 3:61 *LORD, you have heard the vile names they call me. You know all about the plans they have made.*

Lamentations 3:24-26, 30 *I say to myself, "The LORD is my inheritance; therefore, I will hope in him!" The LORD is wonderfully good to those who wait for him and seek him. So it is good to wait quietly for salvation from the LORD. . . . Let them turn the other cheek to those who strike them. Let them accept the insults of their enemies.*
The Lord is aware of any insult that is hurled against us. He will comfort us when we are insulted and reward us for the way in which we respond. Eventually, we will enter a place where there will be no more insults.

How can we avoid insulting others?

1 Peter 3:10 *For the Scriptures say, "If you want a happy life and good days, keep your tongue from speaking evil, and keep your lips from telling lies."*

James 3:2, 5 *We all make many mistakes, but those who control their tongues can also control themselves in every other way. . . . So also, the tongue is a small thing, but what enormous damage it can do.*

We should guard our mouths and carefully watch our words.

Proverbs 10:32 *The godly speak words that are helpful, but the wicked speak only what is corrupt.*

Proverbs 12:6, 18 *The words of the wicked are like a murderous ambush, but the words of the godly save lives. . . . Some people make cutting remarks, but the words of the wise bring healing.*
We should speak nurturing, helpful, and healing words that build up others.

Proverbs 22:10 *Throw out the mocker, and fighting, quarrels, and insults will disappear.*

Proverbs 9:7 *Anyone who rebukes a mocker will get a smart retort. Anyone who rebukes the wicked will get hurt.*
We should avoid association and conversation with those who insult others.

1 Peter 3:8-9 *Finally, all of you should be of one mind, full of sympathy toward each other, loving one another with tender hearts and humble minds. Don't repay evil for evil. Don't retaliate when people say unkind things about you. Instead, pay them back with a blessing. That is what God wants you to do, and he will bless you for it.*
We can receive God's blessing by treating one another with sympathy, tenderheartedness, and humility—not vengeful retaliation.

Proverbs 21:23 *If you keep your mouth shut, you will stay out of trouble.*
Sometimes it is best to remain silent.

PROMISE FROM GOD: 1 Peter 3:9 *Don't retaliate when people say unkind things about you. Instead, pay them back with a blessing. That is what God wants you to do, and he will bless you for it.*

Integrity

How do we develop integrity in our own lives?

Proverbs 16:11 *The LORD demands fairness in every business deal; he sets the standard.*

Proverbs 1:3 *Through these proverbs, people will receive instruction in discipline, good conduct, and doing what is right, just, and fair.*
Look to God in his word—he is the standard of integrity.

Luke 16:10 *Unless you are faithful in small matters, you won't be faithful in large ones. If you cheat even a little, you won't be honest with greater responsibilities.*

2 Corinthians 4:2 *We reject all shameful and underhanded methods. We do not try to trick anyone, and we do not distort the Word of God. We tell the truth before God, and all who are honest know that.*

Numbers 14:24 *But my servant Caleb is different from the others. He has remained loyal to me, and I will bring him into the land he explored. His descendants will receive their full share of that land.*

Live honestly in all your responsibilities and with all people—even when truth is in the minority.

How is integrity evident in our lives?

Daniel 6:4 *Then the other administrators and princes began searching for some fault in the way Daniel was handling his affairs, but they couldn't find anything to criticize. He was faithful and honest and always responsible.*

2 Corinthians 7:2 *Please open your hearts to us. We have not done wrong to anyone. We have not led anyone astray. We have not taken advantage of anyone.*

Titus 2:7-8 *And you yourself must be an example to them by doing good deeds of every kind. Let everything you do reflect the integrity and seriousness of your teaching. Let your teaching be so correct that it can't be criticized. Then those who want to argue will be ashamed because they won't have anything bad to say about us.*

Our integrity is evident in the ways we conduct ourselves and treat others. Our words and actions are to be consistent and above reproach.

Acts 23:1 *Gazing intently at the high council, Paul began: "Brothers, I have always lived before God in all good conscience!"*

Acts 24:16 *I always try to maintain a clear conscience before God and everyone else.*

1 Timothy 1:19 *Cling tightly to your faith in Christ, and always keep your conscience clear. For some people have deliberately violated their consciences; as a result, their faith has been shipwrecked.*
We maintain integrity by keeping our conscience clear before God and others.

PROMISE FROM GOD: Psalm 18:24-25 *The LORD rewarded me for doing right, because of the innocence of my hands in his sight. To the faithful you show yourself faithful; to those with integrity you show integrity.*

Intimacy

see also **Marriage** *and* **Sex/Sexuality**

What must I do to experience an intimate relationship with God?

Genesis 6:9 *This is the history of Noah and his family. Noah was a righteous man, the only blameless man living on earth at the time. He consistently followed God's will and enjoyed a close relationship with him.*

I must live the way God wants me to live.

Psalm 145:18 *The LORD is close to all who call on him, yes, to all who call on him sincerely.*
I must talk with God.

James 4:8 *Draw close to God, and God will draw close to you. Wash your hands, you sinners; purify your hearts, you hypocrites.*
I must stay close to God and purify my heart before him.

Matthew 22:37 *Jesus replied, "You must love the Lord your God with all your heart, all your soul, and all your mind."*
I must love God completely.

Romans 5:11 *So now we can rejoice in our wonderful new relationship with God—all because of what our Lord Jesus Christ has done for us in making us friends of God.*
I must rejoice in God through Christ.

What is the basis for true and lasting intimacy in marriage?

Proverbs 5:15 *Drink water from your own well—share your love only with your wife.*

Proverbs 31:10-11 *Who can find a virtuous and capable wife? She is worth more than precious rubies. Her husband can trust her, and she will greatly enrich his life.*

1 Corinthians 7:3 *The husband should not deprive his wife of sexual intimacy, which is her right as a married woman, nor should the wife deprive her husband.*

Ephesians 5:24-25 *As the church submits to Christ, so you wives must submit to your husbands in everything. And you husbands must love your wives with the same love Christ showed the church. He gave up his life for her.*

True and lasting intimacy in marriage is based on remaining faithful, rejoicing in one another, satisfying each other sexually, recognizing the great value of one's mate, living happily with each other, talking together about spiritual things, and giving thanks to the Lord together.

PROMISE FROM GOD: Psalm 25:14 *Friendship with the LORD is reserved for those who fear him. With them he shares the secrets of his covenant.*

Jealousy

see also Envy

Why is jealousy so dangerous?

Genesis 4:4-5 *The LORD accepted Abel and his offering, but he did not accept Cain and his offering. This made Cain very angry.*

A c t s   1 7 : 5   *But the Jewish leaders were jealous, so they gathered some worthless fellows from the streets to form a mob and start a riot. They attacked the home of Jason, searching for Paul and Silas.*
Jealousy for attention or affection can drive a person to extreme action, even seeking to harm or kill others.

How can jealousy affect our lives?

1   S a m u e l   1 8 : 9 - 1 0   *From that time on Saul kept a jealous eye on David. The very next day, in fact, a tormenting spirit from God overwhelmed Saul.*
Jealousy can open us up to the influence of evil spirits.

1   S a m u e l   1 8 : 1 0 - 1 1   *Saul, who had a spear in his hand, suddenly hurled it at David.*
Saul's jealousy led him to uncontrolled rage.

1   S a m u e l   1 8 : 1 2   *Saul was afraid of him.*
Jealousy brought great fear to Saul. The jealous goal to harm David became Saul's consuming passion.

PROMISE FROM GOD: P r o v e r b s   1 4 : 3 0
A relaxed attitude lengthens life; jealousy rots it away.

Kindness

see also Manners

Why should we be kind to one another?

Ephesians 4:32 *Be kind to each other, tenderhearted, forgiving one another, just as God through Christ has forgiven you.*
We should be kind because God has been kind to us and commands us to be kind to others. It is a way to show others Jesus' love.

Ruth 2:10-11 *"Why are you being so kind to me?" she asked. "I am only a foreigner." "Yes, I know," Boaz replied. "But I also know about the love and kindness you have shown your mother-in-law."*

Matthew 7:12 *Do for others what you would like them to do for you.*
When we are kind, it will encourage kindness in others.

How can we become more kind?

Galatians 5:22 *But when the Holy Spirit controls our lives, he will produce this kind of fruit in us.*
Kindness is a fruit that the Holy Spirit plants in our lives.

1 Corinthians 13:4 *Love is patient and kind.*
From the fountains of love flow rivers of kindness. It is impossible to be truly kind unless we are first truly loving.

PROMISE FROM GOD: Proverbs 11:17
Your own soul is nourished when you are kind.

Listening

see **Communication**

Love

What kind of love does God expect husbands and wives to show to each other?

Song of Songs 8:6-7 *Place me like a seal over your heart. . . . For love is as strong as death.*
Song of Songs is a book about the love husbands and wives should have for each other. True marital love is exclusive and permanent, sealing our hearts in faithfulness to our mate.

Ephesians 5:24-25 *As the church submits to Christ, so you wives must submit to your husbands in everything. And you husbands must love your wives with the same love Christ showed the church. He gave up his life for her.*
After our love for God, nothing should take greater priority than the sacrificial love we have for our mate. This love helps us learn more about how we are to love God, and it is an example to those who are learning about love and about God.

Hebrews 13:4 *Give honor to marriage, and remain faithful to one another in marriage.*
It is essential that before you are married you make a lifetime, irrevocable commitment to stay married. Then, when problems come, you won't be looking for a way out but a way through.

What are some special things that come from a loving relationship?

Proverbs 10:12 *Hatred stirs up quarrels, but love covers all offenses.*

1 Corinthians 13:4-7 *Love is patient and kind. Love is not jealous or boastful or proud or rude. Love does not demand its own way. Love is not irritable, and it keeps no record of when it has been wronged. It is never glad about injustice but rejoices whenever the truth wins out. Love never gives up, never loses faith, is always hopeful, and endures through every circumstance.*
The gifts that come from a loving relationship include forgiveness, patience, kindness, love for truth, love for justice, love for the best in a person, loyalty at any cost, and belief in a person no matter what. Love does not allow for envy, pride, contempt, selfishness, rudeness, a demand for one's own way, irritability, or grudges.

PROMISE FROM GOD: Romans 8:39
Whether we are high above the sky or in the deepest ocean, nothing in all creation will ever be able to separate us from the love of God that is revealed in Christ Jesus our Lord.

Loyalty

see Commitment

Lust

If lust does not involve actual physical behavior, is it wrong?

Luke 11:34 *Your eye is a lamp for your body. A pure eye lets sunshine into your soul.*
When lust is allowed to take up residence in our minds, it tends to consume our thoughts, and the light of God is pushed aside.

1 Kings 11:3 *He had seven hundred wives and three hundred concubines. And sure enough, they led his heart away from the LORD.*
Solomon's lust eventually led to idolatry.

What is the difference between lust and love?

2 Samuel 13:14 *Amnon wouldn't listen to her, and since he was stronger than she was, he raped her.*

185

Lust takes what it wants regardless of the other's needs or desires. Love gives and gives and does not take that which is not offered.

1 Corinthians 13:4-5 *Love is patient and kind. . . . Love does not demand its own way.*
Love is patient and kind. Lust is impatient and rude.

How can I keep my desires from becoming lustful?

Matthew 5:28 *Anyone who even looks at a woman with lust in his eye has already committed adultery with her in his heart.*
We can prevent lust from taking root in our minds by avoiding a "second look."

Philippians 4:8 *Think about things that are pure and lovely and admirable.*
When we fill our hearts and minds with purity and goodness, lust finds no place.

Song of Songs 7:6 *Oh, how delightful you are, my beloved; how pleasant for utter delight!*
When we focus our desires on our mate, lust for others has less room to grow.

PROMISE FROM GOD: Philippians 4:8-9
Fix your thoughts on what is true and honorable and right. Think about things that are pure and lovely and admirable. Think about things that are excellent and

worthy of praise. Keep putting into practice all you
learned from me and heard from me and saw me
doing, and the God of peace will be with you.

Manipulation

How do we recognize manipulation in ourselves and in others?

2 Corinthians 12:16-19 *Some of you admit I*
was not a burden to you. But they still think I was
sneaky and took advantage of you by trickery. But
how? Did any of the men I sent to you take advantage
of you? When I urged Titus to visit you and sent our
other brother with him, did Titus take advantage of
you? No, of course not. . . . Everything we do, dear
friends, is for your benefit.
Manipulators take advantage of others for their
own benefit. Their motive is sinful.

Matthew 7:15 *Beware of false prophets who come*
disguised as harmless sheep, but are really wolves that
will tear you apart.

Galatians 1:7 *You are being fooled by those who*
twist and change the truth concerning Christ.
False prophets and false teachers are often
manipulators. They pretend to have good news
for you, but they are really seeking to take from
you.

Jeremiah 9:5 *They all fool and defraud each other; no one tells the truth. With practiced tongues they tell lies; they wear themselves out with all their sinning.*
Manipulators often use deception. They can make good look evil and evil look good.

Nehemiah 6:9 *They were just trying to intimidate us, imagining that they could break our resolve and stop the work.*
Intimidation is often involved in manipulation. When the manipulator can't entice, he or she may try to intimidate the other into submission.

Judges 14:15-17 *Samson's wife came to him in tears and said, "You don't love me; you hate me! You have given my people a riddle, but you haven't told me the answer." . . . At last, on the seventh day, he told her the answer because of her persistent nagging.*
Emotional pressure and guilt are often used to manipulate.

Proverbs 7:21 *So she seduced him with her pretty speech. With her flattery she enticed him.*

1 Thessalonians 2:5 *Never once did we try to win you with flattery, as you very well know. And God is our witness that we were not just pretending to be your friends so you would give us money!*
Flattery is often used in manipulation. If the manipulator can't openly deceive you, the sweet talk of flattery may do the trick.

PROMISE FROM GOD: Proverbs 14:22
If you plot evil, you will be lost; but if you plan good,
you will be granted unfailing love and faithfulness.

Manners

see also Kindness

Why are good manners important to relationships?

Proverbs 3:3-4 *Never let loyalty and kindness*
get away from you! Wear them like a necklace; write
them deep within your heart. Then you will find favor
with both God and people, and you will gain a good
reputation.
Having good manners brings a good reputation.

1 Peter 3:7 *In the same way, you husbands must*
give honor to your wives. Treat her with
understanding as you live together. . . . If you don't
treat her as you should, your prayers will not be heard.
Having good manners toward our mate benefits
us as well.

Exodus 18:7 *So Moses went out to meet his*
father-in-law. He bowed to him respectfully and
greeted him warmly.
Having good manners helps build stronger family
relationships.

1 Peter 2:12 *Be careful how you live among your unbelieving neighbors. Even if they accuse you of doing wrong, they will see your honorable behavior, and they will believe and give honor to God when he comes to judge the world.*

1 Thessalonians 4:12 *As a result, people who are not Christians will respect the way you live, and you will not need to depend on others to meet your financial needs.*

Having good manners positively affects community life.

How do we develop good manners?

Galations 5:22-23 *But when the Holy Spirit controls our lives, he will produce this kind of fruit in us: love, joy, peace, patience, kindness, goodness, faithfulness, gentleness, and self-control. Here there is no conflict with the law.*

We develop good manners when the Holy Spirit controls our lives.

1 Peter 3:8 *Finally, all of you should be of one mind, full of sympathy toward each other, loving one another with tender hearts and humble minds.*

Matthew 7:12 *Do for others what you would like them to do for you. This is a summary of all that is taught in the law and the prophets.*

We develop good manners when we cultivate a loving, thoughtful attitude toward others.

2 Timothy 3:16 *All Scripture is inspired by God and is useful to teach us what is true and to make us realize what is wrong in our lives. It straightens us out and teaches us to do what is right.*
We develop good manners when we study the Scripture.

Proverbs 20:11 *Even children are known by the way they act, whether their conduct is pure and right.*
We develop good manners in childhood.

Romans 12:13 *When God's children are in need, be the one to help them out. And get into the habit of inviting guests home for dinner or, if they need lodging, for the night.*

Matthew 25:35-36 *I was hungry, and you fed me. I was thirsty, and you gave me a drink. I was a stranger, and you invited me into your home. I was naked, and you gave me clothing. I was sick, and you cared for me. I was in prison, and you visited me.*
We develop good manners when we get into the habit of reaching out to others.

PROMISES FROM GOD: Proverbs 15:1 *A gentle answer turns away wrath, but harsh words stir up anger.*

Proverbs 16:24 *Kind words are like honey—sweet to the soul and healthy for the body.*

Marriage

What kind of relationship should a marriage be?

Genesis 2:18 *And the LORD God said, "It is not good for the man to be alone. I will make a companion who will help him."*

Ecclesiastes 4:9-10 *Two people can accomplish more than twice as much as one. . . . If one person falls, the other can reach out and help.*

1 Corinthians 11:3 *But there is one thing I want you to know: A man is responsible to Christ, a woman is responsible to her husband, and Christ is responsible to God.*

Matthew 19:4-6 *"Haven't you read the Scriptures?" Jesus replied. "They record that from the beginning 'God made them male and female.' And he said, 'This explains why a man leaves his father and mother and is joined to his wife, and the two are united into one.' Since they are no longer two but one, let no one separate them, for God has joined them together."*

Marriage at its best is a relationship so close and intimate that the two work together as one. It involves mutual trust, support, defense, comfort, vulnerability, and responsibility.

What are the keys to a strong, happy marriage?

Joshua 24:15 *Choose today whom you will serve. . . . But as for me and my family, we will serve the LORD.*
A united purpose to serve the Lord promotes a strong, happy marriage.

Proverbs 5:15 *Drink water from your own well—share your love only with your wife.*

Hebrews 13:4 *Give honor to marriage, and remain faithful to one another in marriage. God will surely judge people who are immoral and those who commit adultery.*
Faithfulness promotes trust and intimacy in a marriage.

Matthew 19:6 *Since they are no longer two but one, let no one separate them, for God has joined them together.*
Commitment to the marriage is a prerequisite for making it strong.

Romans 15:2 *We should please others. If we do what helps them, we will build them up in the Lord.*
Self-sacrifice is needed to build up any marriage.

Proverbs 31:31 *Reward her for all she has done. Let her deeds publicly declare her praise.*
A constant desire to affirm each other and enhance each other's value will help the marriage be strong.

1 Corinthians 7:3 *The husband should not deprive his wife of sexual intimacy . . . nor should the wife deprive her husband.*

Song of Songs 1:2, 4, 13 *Kiss me again and again, for your love is sweeter than wine. . . . Bring me into your bedroom, O my king. . . . My lover is like a sachet of myrrh lying between my breasts.*
A healthy sex life is essential to a healthy marriage.

How does God compare marriage to our relationship with him?

Isaiah 54:6 *The LORD has called you back from your grief—as though you were a young wife abandoned by her husband.*

Jeremiah 3:20 *"You have betrayed me. . . . You have been like a faithless wife who leaves her husband," says the LORD.*

2 Corinthians 11:2 *I am jealous for you with the jealousy of God himself. For I promised you as a pure bride to one husband, Christ.*
Our relationship with God, like marriage, is based on mutual love, faithfulness, and permanent commitment.

PROMISE FROM GOD: Ephesians 5:31 *As the Scriptures say, "A man leaves his father and mother and is joined to his wife, and the two are united into one."*

Misunderstandings

What are the dangers of unresolved misunderstandings?

Galatians 2:2 *I went there because God revealed to me that I should go. While I was there I talked privately with the leaders of the church. I wanted them to understand what I had been preaching to the Gentiles. I wanted to make sure they did not disagree, or my ministry would have been useless.*
Unresolved misunderstandings can interfere with serving the Lord.

2 Peter 3:15-17 *Our beloved brother Paul wrote to you with the wisdom God gave him. . . . Some of his comments are hard to understand, and those who are ignorant and unstable have twisted his letters around to mean something quite different from what he meant, just as they do the other parts of Scripture—and the result is disaster for them.*
Unresolved misunderstandings can be disastrous for those involved and for others.

Proverbs 17:14 *Beginning a quarrel is like opening a floodgate, so drop the matter before a dispute breaks out.*
Unresolved misunderstandings can lead to quarrels, which lead to even further friction and damage.

How should we respond to misunderstandings?

1 Corinthians 12:1 *And now, dear brothers and sisters, I will write about the special abilities the Holy Spirit gives to each of us, for I must correct your misunderstandings about them.*

Luke 19:11 *The crowd was listening to everything Jesus said. . . . He told a story to correct the impression that the Kingdom of God would begin right away.*

Joshua 22:12-13 *The whole assembly gathered at Shiloh and prepared to go to war against their brother tribes. First, however, they sent a delegation . . . to talk with the tribes.*
We should have a desire to correct misunderstandings and proactively resolve them.

How can we avoid misunderstandings?

2 Corinthians 1:13 *My letters have been straightforward, and there is nothing written between the lines and nothing you can't understand.*
We should try to be clear with our words.

2 Samuel 20:17 *As he approached, the woman asked, "Are you Joab?" "I am," he replied. So she said, "Listen carefully to your servant." "I'm listening," he said.*

Hebrews 13:22 *I urge you, dear brothers and sisters, please listen carefully to what I have said in this brief letter.*
We can make sure that we listen carefully.

Philippians 3:15 *I hope all of you who are mature Christians will agree on these things. If you disagree on some point, I believe God will make it plain to you.*

Colossians 4:4 *Pray that I will proclaim this message as clearly as I should.*
We can pray for clear understanding for ourselves and for others.

PROMISE FROM GOD:
1 Corinthians 13:12 *Now we see things imperfectly as in a poor mirror, but then we will see everything with perfect clarity. All that I know now is partial and incomplete, but then I will know everything completely, just as God knows me now.*

Money

What is a proper perspective toward money?

Psalm 23:1 *The LORD is my shepherd; I have everything I need.*

Matthew 6:24 *No one can serve two masters. . . . You cannot serve both God and money.*

Mark 8:36 *And how do you benefit if you gain the whole world but lose your own soul in the process?*
Loving money can get our priorities out of line. We must keep reminding ourselves that God must be first in our lives and that money cannot satisfy our deepest needs.

Hebrews 13:5 *Stay away from the love of money; be satisfied with what you have. For God has said, "I will never fail you. I will never forsake you."*

Psalm 119:36 *Give me an eagerness for your decrees; do not inflict me with love for money!*
We should trust God rather than money to provide for our needs.

Proverbs 11:28 *Trust in your money and down you go!*

Isaiah 55:2 *Why spend your money on food that does not give you strength? Listen, and I will tell you where to get food that is good for the soul!*
Too often we buy things to fill a void or a need in our lives. The Bible tells how to acquire a deep and lasting happiness that always satisfies.

Proverbs 19:1 *It is better to be poor and honest than to be a fool and dishonest.*
No amount of money is worthwhile if it is gained deceptively or dishonestly. Taking advantage of others to make money is stealing. Those who do this lose far more than they could ever gain.

Matthew 6:32-33 *Your heavenly Father already knows all your needs, and he will give you all you need from day to day if you live for him and make the Kingdom of God your primary concern.*

Philippians 4:11-12 *For I have learned how to get along happily whether I have much or little. . . . I have learned the secret of living in every situation.*

Philippians 4:19 *And this same God who takes care of me will supply all your needs from his glorious riches.*

The Bible promises that God will supply all of our needs. The problem comes when our definition of "need" is different from God's. The first thing we must do is study God's word to discover what comprises a fulfilling life.

How can we best use our money?

Deuteronomy 16:17 *All must give as they are able, according to the blessings given to them by the LORD your God.*

Proverbs 3:9-10 *Honor the LORD with your wealth and with the best part of everything your land produces. Then he will fill your barns with grain, and your vats will overflow with the finest wine.*

Malachi 3:10 *"Bring all the tithes into the storehouse so there will be enough food in my Temple. If you do," says the LORD Almighty, "I will open the windows of heaven for you. I will pour out a blessing so great you won't have enough room to take it in! Try it! Let me prove it to you!"*

1 Corinthians 16:2 *On every Lord's Day, each of you should put aside some amount of money in relation to what you have earned and save it for this offering.*
We should honor the Lord by giving to his work.

1 John 3:17 *But if one of you has enough money to live well, and sees a brother or sister in need and refuses to help—how can God's love be in that person?*

1 Timothy 6:9, 18 *But people who long to be rich fall into temptation and are trapped by many foolish and harmful desires that plunge them into ruin and destruction. . . . Tell them to use their money to do good. They should be rich in good works and should give generously to those in need, always being ready to share with others whatever God has given them.*
We should use our money to meet others' needs.

PROMISE FROM GOD: 1 Timothy 6:18-19 *They should be rich in good works and should give generously to those in need, always being ready to share with others whatever God has given them. By doing this they will be storing up their treasure as a good foundation for the future so that they may take hold of real life.*

Moving

How can God help us in our move?

Isaiah 41:13 *I am holding you by your right hand—I, the LORD your God. And I say to you, "Do not be afraid. I am here to help you."*

2 Samuel 2:1 *After this, David asked the LORD, "Should I move back to Judah?" And the LORD replied, "Yes." Then David asked, "Which town should I go to?" And the LORD replied, "Hebron."*

Ezra 8:21 *And there by the Ahava Canal, I gave orders for all of us to fast and humble ourselves before our God. We prayed that he would give us a safe journey and protect us, our children, and our goods as we traveled.*

Exodus 33:14-15 *The LORD replied, "I will personally go with you, Moses. I will give you rest—everything will be fine for you." Then Moses said, "If you don't go with us personally, don't let us move a step from this place."*
God will guide us, give us wisdom and courage, and be with us if we ask him.

How can we best handle a move?

Psalm 139:3, 5, 7, 9-10 *You chart the path ahead of me and tell me where to stop and rest. Every moment you know where I am. . . . You both precede and follow me. You place your hand of blessing on my head. . . . I can never escape from your spirit! I can never get away from your presence! . . . If I dwell by the farthest oceans, even there your hand will guide me, and your strength will support me.*

Joshua 1:9 *I command you—be strong and courageous! Do not be afraid or discouraged. For the LORD your God is with you wherever you go.*
When we move to a new place, we should recognize that God is already there—he charts the path ahead and prepares a place for us.

Numbers 10:13 *When the time to move arrived, the LORD gave the order through Moses.*
We should seek to follow the Lord's direction in each move we make.

Genesis 13:18 *Then Abram moved his camp to the oak grove owned by Mamre, which is at Hebron. There he built an altar to the LORD.*
In any move we make, we must continue to worship the Lord regularly.

Proverbs 19:2 *Zeal without knowledge is not good; a person who moves too quickly may go the wrong way.*
Before any move we should pray diligently and think carefully.

PROMISE FROM GOD: Joshua 1:9
The LORD your God is with you wherever you go.

Nagging

Why is nagging so harmful to relationships?

Proverbs 25:24 *It is better to live alone in the corner of an attic than with a contentious wife in a lovely home.*

Proverbs 19:13 *A foolish child is a calamity to a father; a nagging wife annoys like a constant dripping.* There is rarely pleasant fellowship in the company of those who nag.

What are alternatives to nagging?

Galatians 5:25-26 *If we are living now by the Holy Spirit, let us follow the Holy Spirit's leading in every part of our lives. Let us not become conceited, or irritate one another, or be jealous of one another.* We are to follow the Holy Spirit's leading and not irritate one another.

Ephesians 6:4 *And now a word to you fathers. Don't make your children angry by the way you treat them. Rather, bring them up with the discipline and instruction approved by the Lord.* When giving guidance to our children, we are to use the discipline and instruction found in Scripture.

Proverbs 15:1 *A gentle answer turns away wrath, but harsh words stir up anger.*

When giving helpful guidance to others, we are to be gentle and humble.

PROMISE FROM GOD: Galatians 6:1
Dear brothers and sisters, if another Christian is overcome by some sin, you who are godly should gently and humbly help that person back onto the right path.

Needs

How do we keep clear distinctions between needs and wants?

1 Timothy 6:8 *So if we have enough food and clothing, let us be content.*

Philippians 4:11 *Not that I was ever in need, for I have learned how to get along happily whether I have much or little.*

Proverbs 30:8 *Give me neither poverty nor riches! Give me just enough to satisfy my needs.*

Psalm 23:1 *The LORD is my shepherd; I have everything I need.*
When our needs are supplied, we can be content. We will never be content if we focus on our wants and desires, because we always want more.

On whom should we depend to meet our needs?

2 Peter 1:3 *As we know Jesus better, his divine power gives us everything we need for living a godly life.*

Matthew 6:33 *[Your heavenly Father] will give you all you need from day to day if you live for him and make the Kingdom of God your primary concern.*

2 Corinthians 9:8 *God will generously provide all you need. Then you will always have everything you need and plenty left over to share with others.* God will take care of our needs if we live for him and seek his will.

PROMISE FROM GOD:
Philippians 4:19 *And this same God who takes care of me will supply all your needs from his glorious riches, which have been given to us in Christ Jesus.*

Neglect

What can we do when we feel neglected?

Psalm 66:20 *Praise God, who did not ignore my prayer and did not withdraw his unfailing love from me.* Though others may neglect us, God never turns away from us.

James 4:8 *Draw close to God, and God will draw close to you.*

Psalm 68:4, 6 *Rejoice in his presence! . . . God places the lonely in families; he sets the prisoners free and gives them joy.*
When we feel neglected, we must draw near to God. His presence can give us the joy we need.

How do we neglect God? How does our neglect affect our relationships?

Hebrews 2:3 *What makes us think we can escape if we are indifferent to this great salvation that was announced by the Lord Jesus himself?*

Galatians 6:7 *Remember that you can't ignore God and get away with it.*
We neglect God when we ignore his offer of salvation.

Nehemiah 13:11 *I immediately confronted the leaders and demanded, "Why has the Temple of God been neglected?" Then I called all the Levites back again and restored them to their proper duties.*

Hebrews 10:25 *Let us not neglect our meeting together, as some people do, but encourage and warn each other.*
We neglect God when we neglect the church and our responsibility to serve within it.

PROMISE FROM GOD: Hebrews 12:15 *Look after each other so that none of you will miss out on the special favor of God.*

Neighbors

see also Friendship

What are our responsibilities to our neighbors?

Deuteronomy 22:1, 3-4 *If you see your neighbor's ox or sheep wandering away, don't pretend not to see it. Take it back to its owner. . . . Do the same if you find your neighbor's donkey, clothing, or anything else your neighbor loses. Don't pretend you did not see it. If you see your neighbor's ox or donkey lying on the road, do not look the other way. Go and help your neighbor get it to its feet!*

Proverbs 3:28 *If you can help your neighbor now, don't say, "Come back tomorrow, and then I'll help you."*
We should help our neighbors in times of need.

Ephesians 4:25 *Put away all falsehood and "tell your neighbor the truth" because we belong to each other.*
We should tell our neighbors the truth, even when it is painful. This applies also to our spouse and loved ones.

Exodus 20:16 *Do not testify falsely against your neighbor.*
We should not tell lies about our neighbors.

Proverbs 3:29 *Do not plot against your neighbors, for they trust you.*
We should not break our neighbors' trust nor seek to harm our neighbors.

Proverbs 11:12 *It is foolish to belittle a neighbor; a person with good sense remains silent.*
We should not make fun of our neighbors.

Proverbs 27:14 *If you shout a pleasant greeting to your neighbor too early in the morning, it will be counted as a curse!*
We should respect our neighbors' time and privacy.

How should we live among our non-Christian neighbors?

1 Peter 2:12 *Be careful how you live among your unbelieving neighbors. Even if they accuse you of doing wrong, they will see your honorable behavior, and they will believe and give honor to God when he comes to judge the world.*

Colossians 4:5-6 *Live wisely among those who are not Christians, and make the most of every opportunity. Let your conversation be gracious and effective so that you will have the right answer for everyone.*

Galatians 5:14 *The whole law can be summed up in this one command: "Love your neighbor as yourself."*

We should treat our non-Christian neighbors with God's love, live honorably and graciously before them, be an example of godliness, and share God's ways with them.

PROMISE FROM GOD: James 2:8 *Yes indeed, it is good when you truly obey our Lord's royal command found in the Scriptures: "Love your neighbor as yourself."*

Overreact

How does it affect other people when we overreact?

Genesis 34:27, 30 *Then all of Jacob's sons plundered the town because their sister had been defiled there. . . . Afterward Jacob said to Levi and Simeon, "You have made me stink among all the people of this land."*

Exodus 5:7-9 *Do not supply the people with any more straw for making bricks. Let them get it themselves! But don't reduce their production quotas by a single brick. They obviously don't have enough to do. If they did, they wouldn't be talking about going into the wilderness to offer sacrifices to their God. Load them down with more work. Make them sweat! That will teach them.*

Genesis 26:10 *"How could you treat us this way!"* Abimelech exclaimed. *"Someone might have taken your wife and slept with her, and you would have made us guilty of great sin."*
Overreacting can negatively affect others physically, emotionally, and spiritually.

How can we avoid overreacting?

Joshua 22:11-13 *When the rest of Israel heard they had built the altar at Geliloth west of the Jordan River, in the land of Canaan, the whole assembly gathered at Shiloh and prepared to go to war against their brother tribes. First, however, they sent a delegation led by Phinehas.*
We should thoroughly seek to understand the facts before reacting.

James 1:19 *Dear brothers and sisters, be quick to listen, slow to speak, and slow to get angry.*

Proverbs 29:20 *There is more hope for a fool than for someone who speaks without thinking.*
We should be quick to listen and slow to speak. When a verbal reaction is required, we should speak with wisdom and understanding.

1 Peter 2:23 *He did not retaliate when he was insulted. When he suffered, he did not threaten to get even. He left his case in the hands of God, who always judges fairly.*

Proverbs 20:22 *Don't say, "I will get even for this wrong." Wait for the LORD to handle the matter.*

Romans 12:17 *Never pay back evil for evil to anyone. Do things in such a way that everyone can see you are honorable.*
We should avoid reacting vindictively.

Galatians 5:22 *But when the Holy Spirit controls our lives, he will produce this kind of fruit in us: love, joy, peace, patience, kindness, goodness, faithfulness, gentleness, and self-control.*
We should allow the Holy Spirit to control our lives so that we will react with his love, patience, kindness, gentleness, and self-control.

How should we respond to another's overreaction?

Romans 8:28 *And we know that God causes everything to work together for the good of those who love God and are called according to his purpose for them.*

Genesis 50:20 *As far as I am concerned, God turned into good what you meant for evil. He brought me to the high position I have today so I could save the lives of many people.*

1 Samuel 18:13-14 *Finally, Saul banned him from his presence and appointed him commander over only a thousand men, but David faithfully led his troops into battle. David continued to succeed in everything he did, for the LORD was with him.*

We should trust God and be faithful to him in attitude and actions, even when others overreact to what we say or do.

Proverbs 29:8 *Mockers can get a whole town agitated, but those who are wise will calm anger.* We should respond calmly.

Proverbs 22:24-25 *Keep away from angry, short-tempered people, or you will learn to be like them and endanger your soul.*

Proverbs 29:22 *A hot-tempered person starts fights and gets into all kinds of sin.* Avoid spending time with people who consistently overreact.

PROMISE FROM GOD: 2 Peter 1:6 *Knowing God leads to self-control. Self-control leads to patient endurance, and patient endurance leads to godliness.*

Parenting

What does the Bible say about the role of parents?

Deuteronomy 6:6-7 *You must commit yourselves wholeheartedly to these commands I am giving you today. Repeat them again and again to your children.*

2 Timothy 3:15 *You have been taught the holy Scriptures from childhood.*
Parents are to take responsibility for teaching their children the word of God.

Proverbs 3:12 *The LORD corrects those he loves, just as a father corrects a child in whom he delights.*

Hebrews 12:11 *No discipline is enjoyable while it is happening—it is painful! But afterward there will be a quiet harvest of right living.*
Parents are to discipline their children with consistency, wisdom, and love.

Genesis 25:28 *Isaac loved Esau . . . but Rebekah favored Jacob.*
Parents are not to show favoritism between children.

1 Samuel 2:29 *Why do you honor your sons more than me?*
Parents are to honor God. This means doing what God wants for our children, not necessarily what we or they want. Indulgent parents do not help their children develop character.

Luke 15:18-20 *I will go home to my father and say, "Father, I have sinned against both heaven and you, and I am no longer worthy of being called your son. Please take me on as a hired man." So he returned home to his father. And while he was still a*

213

long distance away, his father saw him coming. Filled with love and compassion, he ran to his son, embraced him, and kissed him.
The mark of a loving parent is the willingness to forgive.

PROMISE FROM GOD: Proverbs 22:6 *Teach your children to choose the right path, and when they are older, they will remain upon it.*

Patience

How do we develop patience?

Colossians 1:11 *We also pray that you will be strengthened with his glorious power so that you will have all the patience and endurance you need. May you be filled with joy.*

Galatians 5:22 *But when the Holy Spirit controls our lives, he will produce this kind of fruit in us: love, joy, peace, patience.*

2 Peter 1:6-7 *Self-control leads to patient endurance, and patient endurance leads to godliness. Godliness leads to love for other Christians, and finally you will grow to have genuine love for everyone.*

Romans 15:4 *Such things were written in the Scriptures long ago to teach us. They give us hope and encouragement as we wait patiently for God's promises.*

James 1:3 *For when your faith is tested, your endurance has a chance to grow.*
God develops patience in us through our relationship with him. The more we walk with him, the more we learn his patient endurance.

1 Thessalonians 5:14 *Brothers and sisters, we urge you to . . . be patient with everyone.*

2 Timothy 2:24 *The Lord's servants must not quarrel but must be kind to everyone. They must be able to teach effectively and be patient with difficult people.*

Proverbs 19:11 *People with good sense restrain their anger; they earn esteem by overlooking wrongs.*

Proverbs 14:29 *Those who control their anger have great understanding; those with a hasty temper will make mistakes.*
God uses our relationships with others to develop our patience. Abrasive relationships teach us to endure others patiently.

Romans 5:3-4 *We can rejoice, too, when we run into problems and trials, for we know that they are good for us—they help us learn to endure. And endurance develops strength of character in us, and character strengthens our confident expectation of salvation.*

Romans 12:12 *Be glad for all God is planning for you. Be patient in trouble, and always be prayerful.*

1 Peter 2:19-20 *For God is pleased with you when, for the sake of your conscience, you patiently endure unfair treatment. . . . If you suffer for doing right and are patient beneath the blows, God is pleased with you.*

Ecclesiastes 7:8 *Finishing is better than starting. Patience is better than pride.*
God uses life's circumstances to develop our patience. We cannot always choose the circumstances that come our way, but we can choose the way we respond to them.

What does it mean to "wait on the Lord"?

Isaiah 33:2 *LORD, be merciful to us, for we have waited for you. Be our strength each day and our salvation in times of trouble.*

Isaiah 8:17 *I will wait for the LORD to help us, though he has turned away from the people of Israel. My only hope is in him.*

Psalm 130:5 *I am counting on the LORD; yes, I am counting on him. I have put my hope in his word.*
Waiting on the Lord means bringing our timetable in sync with his. It means relying on him as our source of strength in all situations and maintaining hope in the promises of his word.

Psalm 62:1, 5 *I wait quietly before God, for my salvation comes from him. . . . I wait quietly before God, for my hope is in him.*

216

Psalm 40:1 *I waited patiently for the LORD to help me, and he turned to me and heard my cry.* Waiting on the Lord means quieting our hearts in his presence, trusting him, turning to him for help in trouble, and hoping in him.

Psalm 106:13-14 *Yet how quickly they forgot what he had done! They wouldn't wait for his counsel! In the wilderness, their desires ran wild, testing God's patience in that dry land.*

Acts 1:4 *In one of these meetings as he was eating a meal with them, he told them, "Do not leave Jerusalem until the Father sends you what he promised. Remember, I have told you about this before."*

Psalm 37:34 *Don't be impatient for the LORD to act! Travel steadily along his path. He will honor you, giving you the land. You will see the wicked destroyed.* Waiting on the Lord means waiting for his counsel, his timing, and his settlement of injustices.

Isaiah 30:18 *The LORD still waits for you to come to him so he can show you his love and compassion. For the LORD is a faithful God. Blessed are those who wait for him to help them.*

Lamentations 3:25 *The LORD is wonderfully good to those who wait for him and seek him.* Waiting on the Lord means trusting in his help and seeking his presence.

PROMISE FROM GOD: Isaiah 40:31
Those who wait on the LORD will find new strength.
They will fly high on wings like eagles. They will run
and not grow weary. They will walk and not faint.

Perfect

Does God really expect us to be perfect?

2 Corinthians 7:1 *Because we have these*
promises, dear friends, let us cleanse ourselves from
everything that can defile our body or spirit. And let
us work toward complete purity because we fear God.
As we come to know and revere God, we are
encouraged to aim for the purity of his character
in our own daily choices. To be like our perfect
God is the goal. But as humans, we must
recognize that we will fall far short of perfection.
God knows that.

Philippians 3:12 *I don't mean to say that I*
have already achieved these things or that I have
already reached perfection! But I keep working toward
that day when I will finally be all that Christ Jesus
saved me for and wants me to be.

Ephesians 4:13 *We [will] come to such unity in*
our faith and knowledge of God's Son that we will be
mature and full grown in the Lord, measuring up to
the full stature of Christ.

Our perfection is a process of maturing into pure and godly people. Godliness is becoming more like God, even while falling far short of him. We look forward to a day when that process of reflecting God's nature will be complete.

How should we respond to our own imperfections?

2 Corinthians 7:1 *Because we have these promises, dear friends, let us cleanse ourselves from everything that can defile our body or spirit. And let us work toward complete purity because we fear God.*

1 John 1:8-9 *If we say we have no sin, we are only fooling ourselves and refusing to accept the truth. But if we confess our sins to him, he is faithful and just to forgive us and to cleanse us from every wrong.*

Romans 6:12-13 *Do not let sin control the way you live; do not give in to its lustful desires. . . . Instead, give yourselves completely to God since you have been given new life.*

We must recognize our own sinfulness, while at the same time endeavoring to live more and more like Christ. Because we are growing, we will not make consistently perfect choices. Our goal should be to turn from evil and follow the Lord wholeheartedly in every aspect of our lives.

How should we respond to others' imperfections?

Matthew 7:1, 3, 5 *Stop judging others, and you will not be judged. . . . Why worry about a speck in your friend's eye when you have a log in your own? . . . First get rid of the log from your own eye; then perhaps you will see well enough to deal with the speck in your friend's eye.*

Colossians 3:13 *You must make allowance for each other's faults and forgive the person who offends you. Remember, the Lord forgave you, so you must forgive others.*

1 Peter 3:8 *Finally, all of you should be of one mind, full of sympathy toward each other, loving one another with tender hearts and humble minds.*
We should not respond with critical judgment, but with love, forgiveness, and humility.

PROMISE FROM GOD: Romans 3:23-24 *All have sinned; all fall short of God's glorious standard. Yet now God in his gracious kindness declares us not guilty. He has done this through Christ Jesus, who has freed us by taking away our sins.*

Prayer

What is prayer?

2 Chronicles 7:14 *If my people who are called by my name will humble themselves and pray and seek my face and turn from their wicked ways, I will hear from heaven.*

Prayer is an act of humble worship in which we seek God with all our heart.

Psalm 38:18 *I confess my sins; I am deeply sorry for what I have done.*

1 John 1:9 *If we confess our sins to him, he is faithful and just to forgive us and to cleanse us from every wrong.*
Prayer often begins with confession of sin.

1 Samuel 14:36 *The priest said, "Let's ask God first."*

2 Samuel 5:19 *David asked the LORD, "Should I go out to fight the Philistines?"*
Prayer is asking God for guidance and waiting for his direction.

Mark 1:35 *The next morning Jesus awoke long before daybreak and went out alone into the wilderness to pray.*
Prayer is an intimate relationship with our heavenly Father, who makes his own love and resources available to us.

Psalm 9:1-2 *I will thank you, LORD, with all my heart. . . . I will sing praises to your name, O Most High.*
Through prayer we praise our mighty God.

Does the Bible teach a "right way" to pray?

Nehemiah 1:4 *For days I mourned, fasted, and prayed to the God of heaven.*

Throughout the Bible effective prayer includes elements of adoration, confession, and commitment, as well as requests.

Matthew 6:5-6 *When you pray, don't be like the hypocrites who love to pray publicly on street corners and in the synagogues where everyone can see them. . . . But when you pray, go away by yourself, shut the door behind you, and pray to your Father secretly.* Jesus taught his disciples that prayer is an intimate relationship with the Father that includes a dependency for daily needs, a commitment to obedience, and forgiveness of sin.

Luke 18:1 *One day Jesus told his disciples a story to illustrate their need for constant prayer and to show them that they must never give up.* Prayer is to be consistent and persistent.

Does God always answer prayer?

James 5:16 *Confess your sins to each other and pray for each other so that you may be healed. The earnest prayer of a righteous person has great power and wonderful results.*

1 John 5:14 *We can be confident that he will listen to us whenever we ask him for anything in line with his will.*

We can be confident that God will answer our prayer when we pray from a position of righteousness and submit to his will.

2 Corinthians 12:8 *Three different times I begged the Lord to take it away. Each time he said, ". . . My power works best in your weakness."* Sometimes, like Paul, we will find that God's answer is no.

Exodus 14:15 *Then the LORD said to Moses, "Why are you crying out to me? Tell the people to get moving!"* Our prayer must be accompanied by a willingness to obey.

PROMISE FROM GOD: 1 Peter 3:12 *The eyes of the Lord watch over those who do right, and his ears are open to their prayers.*

Presence

see Absence

Presence of God

How does God's presence in our lives affect our relationships?

Ephesians 4:4 *We are all one body, we have the same Spirit, and we have all been called to the same glorious future.*

1 John 1:7 *If we are living in the light of God's presence, just as Christ is, then we have fellowship with each other, and the blood of Jesus, his Son, cleanses us from every sin.*

Matthew 18:20 *Where two or three gather together because they are mine, I am there among them.*
Because of God's presence in our lives, we have unity, fellowship, and the privilege of prayer with other Christians.

Galatians 5:22-23 *When the Holy Spirit controls our lives, he will produce this kind of fruit in us: love, joy, peace, patience, kindness, goodness, faithfulness, gentleness, and self-control.*
God's presence in our lives fully equips us to demonstrate his nature in our relationships.

Psalm 34:18 *The LORD is close to the brokenhearted; he rescues those who are crushed in spirit.*
When our earthly relationships injure us, God's presence is able to provide comfort, healing, and restoration.

How can we experience God's presence today and for eternity?

James 4:8 *Draw close to God, and God will draw close to you. Wash your hands, you sinners; purify your hearts, you hypocrites.*

Deuteronomy 4:29 *From there you will search again for the LORD your God. And if you search for him with all your heart and soul, you will find him.*

Psalm 145:18 *The LORD is close to all who call on him, yes, to all who call on him sincerely.*
We must draw near to him.

Hebrews 11:6 *It is impossible to please God without faith. Anyone who wants to come to him must believe that there is a God and that he rewards those who sincerely seek him.*

John 3:16 *God so loved the world that he gave his only Son, so that everyone who believes in him will not perish but have eternal life.*
We must have faith in him through Jesus Christ.

Matthew 18:3 *Then he said, "I assure you, unless you turn from your sins and become as little children, you will never get into the Kingdom of Heaven."*
We must turn from our sins, ask God to forgive us for our sins, and trust Jesus to be Lord of our life.

John 14:23 *Jesus replied, "All those who love me will do what I say. My Father will love them, and we will come to them and live with them."*

Psalm 16:11 *You will show me the way of life, granting me the joy of your presence and the pleasures of living with you forever.*

God's solution to our sinfulness is for us to come to him by faith—by believing and accepting Jesus' payment for our sin, turning from our sin, and obeying God.

How can we be assured of God's presence?

Psalm 23:6 *Surely your goodness and unfailing love will pursue me all the days of my life, and I will live in the house of the LORD forever.*

Psalm 139:5, 7 *You both precede and follow me. You place your hand of blessing on my head. . . . I can never escape from your spirit! I can never get away from your presence!*

Romans 8:35, 38-39 *Can anything ever separate us from Christ's love? . . . I am convinced that nothing can ever separate us from his love. Death can't, and life can't. The angels can't, and the demons can't. Our fears for today, our worries about tomorrow, and even the powers of hell can't keep God's love away. Whether we are high above the sky or in the deepest ocean, nothing in all creation will ever be able to separate us from the love of God that is revealed in Christ Jesus our Lord.*

Once we have a relationship with God, his presence is always with us. He promises that nothing can separate us from his love.

John 14:16-17 *I will ask the Father, and he will give you another Counselor, who will never leave you. He is the Holy Spirit, who leads into all truth.*

2 Corinthians 1:22 *He has identified us as his own by placing the Holy Spirit in our hearts as the first installment of everything he will give us.*
When we trust in God through Christ, he gives us his Spirit as our constant companion and guide. The Holy Spirit in our hearts assures us that God is with us and will keep us with him forever.

Psalm 9:9-10 *The LORD is a shelter for the oppressed, a refuge in times of trouble. Those who know your name trust in you, for you, O LORD, have never abandoned anyone who searches for you.*

Psalm 34:18-19 *The LORD is close to the brokenhearted; he rescues those who are crushed in spirit. The righteous face many troubles, but the LORD rescues them from each and every one.*

Matthew 28:20 *"Teach these new disciples to obey all the commands I have given you. And be sure of this: I am with you always, even to the end of the age."*
Those who trust in God always have his presence with them regardless of life's circumstances.

PROMISE FROM GOD: Psalm 16:8, 11
I know the LORD is always with me. I will not be shaken, for he is right beside me. . . . You will show me the way of life, granting me the joy of your presence and the pleasures of living with you forever.

Pressure

How can we best handle pressure?

Mark 14:33-36 *He took Peter, James, and John with him, and he began to be filled with horror and deep distress. He told them, "My soul is crushed with grief to the point of death. Stay here and watch with me." He went on a little farther and fell face down on the ground. He prayed that, if it were possible, the awful hour awaiting him might pass him by. "Abba, Father," he said, "everything is possible for you. Please take this cup of suffering away from me. Yet I want your will, not mine."*
We should follow Jesus' example of praying to our Father in heaven, relying on his strength, and submitting to his will.

Psalm 119:143 *As pressure and stress bear down on me, I find joy in your commands.*
Life's pressures give us an opportunity to obey God's commands. When we do, we will find true joy.

Psalm 62:1-2 *I wait quietly before God, for my salvation comes from him. He alone is my rock and my salvation, my fortress where I will never be shaken.*

1 Samuel 30:6 *David was now in serious trouble because his men were very bitter about losing their wives and children, and they began to talk of stoning him. But David found strength in the LORD his God.* We should focus on God's power and ability to solve our problems. God will give us the strength to be successful.

Exodus 18:17-18, 24-26 *"This is not good!" his father-in-law exclaimed. "You're going to wear yourself out—and the people, too. This job is too heavy a burden for you to handle all by yourself." . . . Moses listened to his father-in-law's advice and followed his suggestions. He chose capable men from all over Israel and made them judges over the people. . . . They brought the hard cases to Moses, but they judged the smaller matters themselves.*
We should listen to godly counsel. Delegation is often a good solution to the mounting pressure we feel from trying to do everything ourselves.

Daniel 1:8 *Daniel made up his mind not to defile himself by eating the food and wine given to them by the king. He asked the chief official for permission to eat other things instead.*

Genesis 39:9-10 *"How could I ever do such a wicked thing? It would be a great sin against God." She kept putting pressure on him day after day, but he refused to sleep with her, and he kept out of her way as much as possible.*
Temptation can best be handled by acknowledging it as sin and standing firm in our convictions and commitment to God. Standing firm can sometimes mean running away.

2 Corinthians 4:8-10 *We are pressed on every side by troubles, but we are not crushed and broken. We are perplexed, but we don't give up and quit. We are hunted down, but God never abandons us. We get knocked down, but we get up again and keep going. Through suffering, these bodies of ours constantly share in the death of Jesus so that the life of Jesus may also be seen in our bodies.*
God never abandons us when we are under pressure. Instead, pressure can give us even closer fellowship with Jesus.

Psalm 55:22 *Give your burdens to the LORD, and he will take care of you. He will not permit the godly to slip and fall.*

Matthew 11:28 *Then Jesus said, "Come to me, all of you who are weary and carry heavy burdens, and I will give you rest."*

1 Peter 5:7 *Give all your worries and cares to God, for he cares about what happens to you.*

Philippians 4:6-7 *Don't worry about anything; instead, pray about everything. Tell God what you need, and thank him for all he has done. If you do this, you will experience God's peace, which is far more wonderful than the human mind can understand.* Letting God carry our burdens can relieve the pressure and help us to endure.

How can we respond to others who are under pressure?

Philippians 2:4 *Don't think only about your own affairs, but be interested in others, too, and what they are doing.* We should never be so preoccupied that we become insensitive to the pressures others face. As we help others handle their pressures, it may relieve our own.

Genesis 25:32-33 *"Look, I'm dying of starvation!" said Esau. "What good is my birthright to me now?" So Jacob insisted, "Well then, swear to me right now that it is mine." So Esau swore an oath, thereby selling all his rights as the firstborn to his younger brother.* We should not take advantage of others when they are under pressure.

Are there ways to prevent pressure?

Isaiah 33:2 *LORD, be merciful to us, for we have waited for you. Be our strength each day and our salvation in times of trouble.*

231

The Lord wants to give us strength every day, not just in times of trouble.

1 Kings 22:13-14 *The messenger who went to get Micaiah said to him, "Look, all the prophets are promising victory for the king. Be sure that you agree with them and promise success." But Micaiah replied, "As surely as the LORD lives, I will say only what the LORD tells me to say."*
We should determine to be faithful to God before times of pressure come. It is much harder to make that decision after the pressure is already on.

1 Corinthians 15:33 *Don't be fooled by those who say such things, for "bad company corrupts good character."*

Psalm 1:1 *Oh, the joys of those who do not follow the advice of the wicked, or stand around with sinners, or join in with scoffers.*
We should choose godly companions and counselors.

PROMISE FROM GOD: Psalm 62:1-2 *I wait quietly before God, for my salvation comes from him. He alone is my rock and my salvation, my fortress where I will never be shaken.*

Priorities

How do we set good priorities?

Deuteronomy 10:12-13 *What does the LORD your God require of you? He requires you to fear him, to live according to his will, to love and worship him with all your heart and soul, and to obey the LORD's commands.*
There can be no greater priority than loving and obeying God.

Matthew 6:33 *He will give you all you need from day to day if you live for him and make the Kingdom of God your primary concern.*
Helping others come to faith in Christ should be our highest priority.

How can we measure our priorities?

Proverbs 3:5-6 *Trust in the LORD with all your heart; do not depend on your own understanding. Seek his will in all you do, and he will direct your paths.*

Luke 12:34 *Wherever your treasure is, there your heart and thoughts will also be.*

Exodus 20:3 *Do not worship any other gods besides me.*

Joshua 24:15 *If you are unwilling to serve the LORD, then choose today whom you will serve. . . . But as for me and my family, we will serve the LORD.*

If God is the center of our lives, our relationship with him will be our highest priority. Priorities are scales on which our love for God is weighed. We focus most on what or whom we love most.

PROMISE FROM GOD: Proverbs 3:6
Seek his will in all you do, and he will direct your paths.

Problems

see also **Conflict**

How does God view our problems?

1 Peter 5:7 *Give all your worries and cares to God, for he cares about what happens to you.*
God cares about us and our problems.

Psalm 145:14 *The LORD helps the fallen and lifts up those bent beneath their loads.*
God helps us with our problems.

Acts 8:4 *The believers who had fled Jerusalem went everywhere preaching the Good News about Jesus.*

Philippians 1:12-14 *I want you to know, dear brothers and sisters, that everything that has happened to me here has helped to spread the Good News. For everyone here, including all the soldiers in the palace guard, knows that I am in chains because of Christ. And because of my imprisonment, many of the Christians here have gained confidence and become more bold in telling others about Christ.*

Romans 8:28 *And we know that God causes everything to work together for the good of those who love God and are called according to his purpose for them.*

God can work his purposes in our lives through the problems we experience.

How can we prepare for problems?

Colossians 2:6-7 *Just as you accepted Christ Jesus as your Lord, you must continue to live in obedience to him. Let your roots grow down into him and draw up nourishment from him, so you will grow in faith, strong and vigorous in the truth you were taught. Let your lives overflow with thanksgiving for all he has done.*

Jude 1:20-21 *You, dear friends, must continue to build your lives on the foundation of your holy faith. And continue to pray as you are directed by the Holy Spirit. Live in such a way that God's love can bless you as you wait for the eternal life that our Lord Jesus Christ in his mercy is going to give you.*

Ephesians 6:10-12 *Be strong with the Lord's mighty power. Put on all of God's armor so that you will be able to stand firm against all strategies and tricks of the Devil. For we are not fighting against people made of flesh and blood, but against the evil rulers and authorities of the unseen world, against those mighty powers of darkness who rule this world, and against wicked spirits in the heavenly realms.* We can best prepare for life's problems by living lives of faith, love, obedience and prayer. Then we will be strong with God's power. If we go onto life's battlefields already equipped with God's spiritual armor, we will more quickly and easily win the battles that our problems bring. The heat of battle is no time to be looking for armor and putting it on.

How should we cope with life's problems when they come?

Philippians 4:6 *Don't worry about anything; instead, pray about everything. Tell God what you need, and thank him for all he has done.*

Psalm 56:3-4 *When I am afraid, I put my trust in you. O God, I praise your word. I trust in God, so why should I be afraid? What can mere mortals do to me?* As we face problems, our response should be to turn to God in trust and prayer.

Psalm 119:24 *Your decrees please me; they give me wise advice.*

Proverbs 6:22 *Wherever you walk, their counsel can lead you. When you sleep, they will protect you. When you wake up in the morning, they will advise you.*

When we face problems, God's word is the best source of wise advice.

Acts 16:22-25 *A mob quickly formed against Paul and Silas, and the city officials ordered them stripped and beaten with wooden rods. They were severely beaten, and then they were thrown into prison. . . . Around midnight, Paul and Silas were praying and singing hymns to God, and the other prisoners were listening.*

James 1:2 *Dear brothers and sisters, whenever trouble comes your way, let it be an opportunity for joy.*
We can respond to our problems with faith, praise, and joy in God.

PROMISE FROM GOD: Philippians 4:6 *Don't worry about anything; instead, pray about everything. Tell God what you need, and thank him for all he has done.*

Prosperity

see **Money**

Quarreling

see also **Conflict, Differences,** *and* **Disagreement**

How is quarreling harmful to relationships?

Proverbs 10:12 *Hatred stirs up quarrels, but love covers all offenses.*

Genesis 16:5 *Then Sarai said to Abram, "It's all your fault!"*

1 Corinthians 3:3 *You are jealous of one another and quarrel with each other. Doesn't that prove you are controlled by your own desires? You are acting like people who don't belong to the Lord.*

James 4:2 *You are jealous for what others have, and you can't possess it, so you fight and quarrel to take it away from them.*
Quarreling is often a symptom of weaknesses in a relationship; it may signify hatred, anger, jealousy, pride, or immaturity.

Mark 3:24 *A kingdom at war with itself will collapse.*

2 Timothy 2:14 *Command them in God's name to stop fighting over words. Such arguments are useless, and they can ruin those who hear them.*

Proverbs 25:24 *It is better to live alone in the corner of an attic than with a contentious wife in a lovely home.*

Quarreling can destroy unity, make companionship unpleasant, cause estrangement, and even destroy lives.

How can we avoid quarreling?

Romans 12:18 *Do your part to live in peace with everyone, as much as possible.*

1 Corinthians 1:10 *Now, dear brothers and sisters, I appeal to you by the authority of the Lord Jesus Christ to stop arguing among yourselves. Let there be real harmony so there won't be divisions in the church. I plead with you to be of one mind, united in thought and purpose.*

Ephesians 4:3 *Always keep yourselves united in the Holy Spirit, and bind yourselves together with peace.*
Making harmony and peace a priority in our relationships will help keep us from quarreling over less important matters.

2 Timothy 2:24-25 *The Lord's servants must not quarrel but must be kind to everyone. They must be able to teach effectively and be patient with difficult people. They should gently teach those who oppose the truth.*

Proverbs 15:1 *A gentle answer turns away wrath, but harsh words stir up anger.*
To avoid quarrels, our manner should be gentle, humble, kind, patient, and even-tempered.

Proverbs 17:14 *Beginning a quarrel is like opening a floodgate, so drop the matter before a dispute breaks out.*

Romans 14:1 *Accept Christians who are weak in faith, and don't argue with them about what they think is right or wrong.*
We can accept others without always agreeing with them.

Romans 16:17 *Watch out for people who cause divisions and upset people's faith by teaching things that are contrary to what you have been taught. Stay away from them.*

Proverbs 22:10 *Throw out the mocker, and fighting, quarrels, and insults will disappear.*
We can choose wisely the company we keep. Spending time with quarrelsome people will eventually bring us strife.

PROMISES FROM GOD: Matthew 5:9 *God blesses those who work for peace, for they will be called the children of God.*

James 3:18 *And those who are peacemakers will plant seeds of peace and reap a harvest of goodness.*

Reconciliation

see also **Forgiveness**

What does the Bible say about reconciliation with others?

Matthew 5:23-24 *If you are standing before the altar in the Temple, offering a sacrifice to God, and you suddenly remember that someone has something against you, leave your sacrifice there beside the altar. Go and be reconciled to that person. Then come and offer your sacrifice to God.*

Being reconciled with other people is important to our relationship with God.

Matthew 5:25-26 *Come to terms quickly with your enemy before it is too late and you are dragged into court, handed over to an officer, and thrown in jail. I assure you that you won't be free again until you have paid the last penny.*

Working for reconciliation with others is in our own best interest.

Matthew 18:15 *If another believer sins against you, go privately and point out the fault. If the other person listens and confesses it, you have won that person back.*

God wants us to resolve our differences with others.

Genesis 33:8 *"What were all the flocks and herds I met as I came?" Esau asked. Jacob replied, "They are gifts, my lord, to ensure your goodwill."*

Proverbs 21:14 *A secret gift calms anger.*
Giving gifts can be an important part of being reconciled with other people.

Ephesians 2:14 *Christ himself has made peace between us Jews and you Gentiles by making us all one people. He has broken down the wall of hostility that used to separate us.*
In Christ, God has made a way for groups at enmity with one another to make peace and be fully reconciled.

Why is restitution important in relationships?

Numbers 5:7 *They must confess their sin and make full restitution for what they have done, adding a penalty of 20 percent and returning it to the person who was wronged.*
Restitution acknowledges that the other person has been wronged. It upholds God's justice. Acknowledging one's faults and restoring what has been lost help heal the relationship.

PROMISE FROM GOD: Jeremiah 3:22 *Come back to me, and I will heal your wayward hearts.*

Refreshment

What refreshes the soul?

Proverbs 11:25 *Those who refresh others will themselves be refreshed.*
Ministering to others refreshes the soul.

Psalm 133:1, 3 *How wonderful it is, how pleasant, when brothers live together in harmony!*

Harmony is as refreshing as the dew from Mount Hermon that falls on the mountains of Zion. And the LORD has pronounced his blessing, even life forevermore.
Harmonious relationships refresh the soul.

What refreshes the mind?

Hebrews 8:10 *This is the new covenant I will make with the people of Israel on that day, says the Lord: I will put my laws in their minds so they will understand them, and I will write them on their hearts so they will obey them. I will be their God, and they will be my people.*

Romans 12:2 *Don't copy the behavior and customs of this world, but let God transform you into a new person by changing the way you think. Then you will know what God wants you to do, and you will know how good and pleasing and perfect his will really is.*

243

God's word refreshes and renews our minds.

Ephesians 4:22-24 *Throw off your old evil nature and your former way of life, which is rotten through and through. . . . Instead, there must be a spiritual renewal of your thoughts and attitudes. You must display a new nature because you are a new person, created in God's likeness—righteous, holy, and true.*

Romans 8:5 *Those who are dominated by the sinful nature think about sinful things, but those who are controlled by the Holy Spirit think about things that please the Spirit.*
The presence of the Holy Spirit in our lives renews our mind.

PROMISE FROM GOD: Proverbs 11:25 *Those who refresh others will themselves be refreshed.*

Relationships

see also **Friendship** *and* **Marriage**

How can we build a healthy marriage relationship?

Genesis 2:18 *And the LORD God said, "It is not good for the man to be alone. I will make a companion who will help him."*
We can spend time enjoying the companionship of our mate.

1 Corinthians 13:4-7 *Love is patient and kind. Love is not jealous or boastful or proud or rude. Love does not demand its own way. Love is not irritable, and it keeps no record of when it has been wronged. It is never glad about injustice but rejoices whenever the truth wins out. Love never gives up, never loses faith, is always hopeful, and endures through every circumstance.*

Ephesians 5:33 *Each man must love his wife as he loves himself, and the wife must respect her husband.*

1 Peter 3:7 *You husbands must give honor to your wives. Treat her with understanding as you live together. She may be weaker than you are, but she is your equal partner in God's gift of new life. If you don't treat her as you should, your prayers will not be heard.*

Hebrews 13:4 *Give honor to marriage, and remain faithful to one another in marriage. God will surely judge people who are immoral and those who commit adultery.*
A marriage should be based on love, respect, faithfulness, and honor.

Ecclesiastes 4:9-11 *Two people can accomplish more than twice as much as one; they get a better return for their labor. If one person falls, the other can reach out and help. But people who are alone when they fall are in real trouble. And on a cold*

night, two under the same blanket can gain warmth from each other. But how can one be warm alone?
Working together and helping one another are important in building a strong marriage.

1 Corinthians 11:3 *A man is responsible to Christ, a woman is responsible to her husband, and Christ is responsible to God.*
Marriage should operate under God's authority and his designated responsibility chain.

Proverbs 5:18-19 *Let your wife be a fountain of blessing for you. Rejoice in the wife of your youth. She is a loving doe, a graceful deer. Let her breasts satisfy you always. May you always be captivated by her love.*

Song of Songs 2:16 *My lover is mine, and I am his. He feeds among the lilies!*
A strong sexual relationship is an important element of the marriage relationship.

How can we restore broken relationships?

Luke 15:18 *I will go home to my father and say, "Father, I have sinned against both heaven and you."*
We may need to confess to others that we have wronged them.

Matthew 18:15 *If another believer sins against you, go privately and point out the fault. If the other person listens and confesses it, you have won that person back.*

We may need to confront another in order to restore a relationship.

Ephesians 4:26, 31-32 *"Don't sin by letting anger gain control over you." Don't let the sun go down while you are still angry. . . . Get rid of all bitterness, rage, anger, harsh words, and slander, as well as all types of malicious behavior. Instead, be kind to each other, tenderhearted, forgiving one another, just as God through Christ has forgiven you.* We should deal with our own anger and forgive others.

Genesis 50:18-21 *Then his brothers came and bowed low before him. "We are your slaves," they said. But Joseph told them, "Don't be afraid of me. Am I God, to judge and punish you? As far as I am concerned, God turned into good what you meant for evil. He brought me to the high position I have today so I could save the lives of many people. No, don't be afraid. Indeed, I myself will take care of you and your families." And he spoke very kindly to them, reassuring them.*

Colossians 3:13 *You must make allowance for each other's faults and forgive the person who offends you. Remember, the Lord forgave you, so you must forgive others.*
To restore a broken relationship, we need to forgive and not hold grudges or seek revenge.

PROMISE FROM GOD: Romans 5:11
We can rejoice in our wonderful new relationship with God—all because of what our Lord Jesus Christ has done for us in making us friends of God.

Respect

Whom should we honor and respect?

Exodus 3:5 *"Do not come any closer," God told him. "Take off your sandals, for you are standing on holy ground."*

1 Samuel 12:24 *Be sure to fear the LORD and sincerely worship him. Think of all the wonderful things he has done for you.*
We must honor and respect God above all else.

Ephesians 5:33 *Each man must love his wife as he loves himself, and the wife must respect her husband.*

1 Peter 3:7 *You husbands must give honor to your wives. Treat her with understanding as you live together . . . she is your equal partner in God's gift of new life. If you don't treat her as you should, your prayers will not be heard.*
We must treat our spouse with utmost honor and respect.

Exodus 20:12 *Honor your father and mother. Then you will live a long, full life in the land the LORD your God will give you.*

One of God's Ten Commandments is that we treat our parents with honor and respect.

1 Thessalonians 5:12-13 *Dear brothers and sisters, honor those who are your leaders in the Lord's work. . . . Think highly of them and give them your wholehearted love because of their work.*
We must treat our spiritual leaders with honor and respect.

Leviticus 19:32 *Show your fear of God by standing up in the presence of elderly people and showing respect for the aged.*
The elderly are worthy of our respect.

Exodus 22:28 *Do not blaspheme God or curse anyone who rules over you.*

Ecclesiastes 10:20 *Never make light of the king, even in your thoughts. And don't make fun of a rich man, either. A little bird may tell them what you have said.*

1 Samuel 24:6 *It is a serious thing to attack the* LORD*'s anointed one.*
We should treat those who have authority and power with respect.

Ephesians 6:5, 9 *Slaves, obey your earthly masters with deep respect and fear. Serve them sincerely as you would serve Christ. . . . And in the same way, you masters must treat your slaves right.*

Don't threaten them; remember, you both have the same Master in heaven, and he has no favorites.
Employers and employees should treat each other with respect.

1 Peter 2:17 *Show respect for everyone. Love your Christian brothers and sisters. Fear God. Show respect for the king.*
We must treat all people with respect.

How do we gain respect?

Jude 1:20 *You, dear friends, must continue to build your lives on the foundation of your holy faith.*

Matthew 7:12 *Do for others what you would like them to do for you.*

Romans 2:10 *There will be glory and honor and peace from God for all who do good.*
We gain respect in much the same way that we show it—building our lives on God's word, treating others the way we would like to be treated, and standing up for truth no matter what.

PROMISE FROM GOD: Revelation 4:11 *You are worthy, O Lord our God, to receive glory and honor and power. For you created everything, and it is for your pleasure that they exist and were created.*

Responsibility

What are our primary responsibilities before God?

Micah 6:8 *O people, the Lord has already told you what is good, and this is what he requires: to do what is right, to love mercy, and to walk humbly with your God.*

We are to have a personal relationship with the living God. We are to have loving, merciful relationships with others. We are to be obedient to God as we make right choices in our daily lives.

How do we develop responsibility?

Matthew 25:20-21 *The servant to whom he had entrusted the five bags of gold said, "Sir, you gave me five bags of gold to invest, and I have doubled the amount." The master was full of praise. "Well done, my good and faithful servant. You have been faithful in handling this small amount, so now I will give you many more responsibilities. Let's celebrate together!"*

Galatians 6:5 *We are each responsible for our own conduct.*

We develop responsibility by conscientiously doing what is right and fulfilling the duties that are given to us.

Proverbs 3:11-12 *My child, don't ignore it when the LORD disciplines you, and don't be discouraged when he corrects you. For the LORD corrects those he loves, just as a father corrects a child in whom he delights.*

Hebrews 12:11 *No discipline is enjoyable while it is happening—it is painful! But afterward there will be a quiet harvest of right living for those who are trained in this way.*

You will be more responsible if you submit to God's discipline and let him work in your heart and life.

PROMISE FROM GOD: Matthew 25:29 *To those who use well what they are given, even more will be given, and they will have an abundance. But from those who are unfaithful, even what little they have will be taken away.*

Restitution

see **Reconciliation**

Retirement

What does the Bible say about retirement?

Deuteronomy 34:7 *Moses was 120 years old when he died, yet his eyesight was clear, and he was as strong as ever.*

Joshua 14:10-11 *Now, as you can see, the
LORD has kept me alive and well as he promised for
all these forty-five years since Moses made this
promise—even while Israel wandered in the
wilderness. Today I am eighty-five years old. I am as
strong now as I was when Moses sent me on that
journey, and I can still travel and fight as well as I
could then.*
The Bible does not give an age for retirement,
with the exception of the Levites who served in
the Tabernacle (Num. 8:24-25).

Joshua 13:1 *When Joshua was an old man, the
LORD said to him, "You are growing old, and much
land remains to be conquered."*

Numbers 20:26 *There you will remove Aaron's
priestly garments and put them on Eleazar, his son.
Aaron will die there and join his ancestors.*
It is good to plan for succession before the day
comes when the successor is needed.

Ecclesiastes 6:1-2 *There is another serious
tragedy I have seen in our world. God gives great
wealth and honor to some people and gives them
everything they could ever want, but then he doesn't
give them the health to enjoy it. They die, and others
get it all! This is meaningless—a sickening tragedy.*
Realizing that we all eventually die, we are wise
to plan for the distribution of our wealth to those
we leave behind.

How can we best transition to retirement?

Isaiah 46:4 *I will be your God throughout your lifetime—until your hair is white with age. I made you, and I will care for you. I will carry you along and save you.*
Our relationship with God should continue to grow as we age.

Proverbs 16:31 *Gray hair is a crown of glory; it is gained by living a godly life.*
Recognizing the benefits of a godly life can help us grow older gracefully.

Proverbs 17:6 *Grandchildren are the crowning glory of the aged; parents are the pride of their children.*
One of the most important aspects of life, relationships, continues through retirement. Focusing on our relationships can make our golden years truly golden.

How can we continue to be productive in our retirement years?

Hebrews 6:11-12 *Our great desire is that you will keep right on loving others as long as life lasts, in order to make certain that what you hope for will come true. Then you will not become spiritually dull and indifferent. Instead, you will follow the example of those who are going to inherit God's promises because of their faith and patience.*

We can be productive by loving others.

Psalm 92:12-15 *But the godly will flourish like palm trees and grow strong like the cedars of Lebanon. For they are transplanted into the Lord's own house. They flourish in the courts of our God. Even in old age they will still produce fruit; they will remain vital and green. They will declare, "The LORD is just! He is my rock! There is nothing but goodness in him!"*

Titus 2:1, 3-4 *But as for you, promote the kind of living that reflects right teaching. . . . Teach others what is good. These older women must train the younger women to love their husbands and their children.*
We can be productive by living godly lives and teaching others to do the same.

Numbers 8:25-26 *They must retire at the age of fifty. After retirement they may assist their fellow Levites by performing guard duty at the Tabernacle, but they may not officiate in the service. This is how you will assign duties to the Levites.*
We can be productive by being flexible to changes in our roles.

Proverbs 20:29 *The glory of the young is their strength; the gray hair of experience is the splendor of the old.*

Job 12:12-13 *Wisdom belongs to the aged, and understanding to those who have lived many years. But true wisdom and power are with God; counsel and understanding are his.*
We can be productive by using our wisdom and understanding as gifts from God to help others.

PROMISE FROM GOD: Psalm 119:54
Your principles have been the music of my life throughout the years of my pilgrimage.

Roles

What is the role of a man in his marriage?

Malachi 2:14-16 *You cry out, "Why has the LORD abandoned us?" I'll tell you why! Because the LORD witnessed the vows you and your wife made to each other on your wedding day when you were young. But you have been disloyal to her, though she remained your faithful companion, the wife of your marriage vows. Didn't the LORD make you one with your wife? In body and spirit you are his. And what does he want? Godly children from your union. So guard yourself; remain loyal to the wife of your youth. "For I hate divorce!" says the LORD, the God of Israel. "It is as cruel as putting on a victim's bloodstained coat," says the LORD Almighty. "So guard yourself; always remain loyal to your wife."*

1 Corinthians 7:11 *The husband must not leave his wife.*

Ecclesiastes 9:9 *Live happily with the woman you love through all the meaningless days of life that God has given you in this world. The wife God gives you is your reward for all your earthly toil.*

Proverbs 5:15-19 *Drink water from your own well—share your love only with your wife. Why spill the water of your springs in public, having sex with just anyone? You should reserve it for yourselves. Don't share it with strangers. Let your wife be a fountain of blessing for you. Rejoice in the wife of your youth. She is a loving doe, a graceful deer. Let her breasts satisfy you always. May you always be captivated by her love.*

The husband should be a faithful, loving, contented, intimate partner for his wife.

Ephesians 5:25, 28-29, 33 *You husbands must love your wives with the same love Christ showed the church. He gave up his life for her. . . . In the same way, husbands ought to love their wives as they love their own bodies. For a man is actually loving himself when he loves his wife. No one hates his own body but lovingly cares for it, just as Christ cares for his body, which is the church. . . . So again I say, each man must love his wife as he loves himself.*

Colossians 3:19 *You husbands must love your wives and never treat them harshly.*

The husband's love for his wife should mirror
Jesus' love for his church.

1 P e t e r 3 : 7 *You husbands must give honor to
your wives. Treat her with understanding as you live
together. She may be weaker than you are, but she is
your equal partner in God's gift of new life. If you
don't treat her as you should, your prayers will not be
heard.*
The husband should treat his wife with honor
and understanding.

E p h e s i a n s 5 : 2 3 *A husband is the head of his
wife as Christ is the head of his body, the church; he
gave his life to be her Savior.*

1 C o r i n t h i a n s 1 1 : 3 *A man is responsible to
Christ, a woman is responsible to her husband, and
Christ is responsible to God.*
The husband is responsible to God in his role as
the leader of his family.

What is the role of a woman in her marriage?

G e n e s i s 2 : 1 8 , 2 4 *The LORD God said, "It is not
good for the man to be alone. I will make a
companion who will help him." . . . This explains why
a man leaves his father and mother and is joined to
his wife, and the two are united into one.*

1 C o r i n t h i a n s 7 : 3 9 *A wife is married to her
husband as long as he lives.*

258

The wife should be a faithful, loving, contented, intimate partner for her husband.

1 Peter 3:1-2 *You wives must accept the authority of your husbands, even those who refuse to accept the Good News. Your godly lives will speak to them better than any words. They will be won over by watching your pure, godly behavior.*

Ephesians 5:22-24 *You wives will submit to your husbands as you do to the Lord. For a husband is the head of his wife as Christ is the head of his body, the church; he gave his life to be her Savior. As the church submits to Christ, so you wives must submit to your husbands in everything.*

A wife should trust God and accept the authority God has given her husband.

Proverbs 31:10-12 *Who can find a virtuous and capable wife? She is worth more than precious rubies. Her husband can trust her, and she will greatly enrich his life. She will not hinder him but help him all her life.*

Proverbs 12:4 *A worthy wife is her husband's joy and crown; a shameful wife saps his strength.*

Proverbs 18:22 *The man who finds a wife finds a treasure and receives favor from the LORD.*

Proverbs 19:14 *Parents can provide their sons with an inheritance of houses and wealth, but only the LORD can give an understanding wife.*

A godly wife helps her husband and family.

What is the role of a man in his family?

1 Timothy 5:8 *Those who won't care for their own relatives, especially those living in the same household, have denied what we believe. Such people are worse than unbelievers.*
A man should provide for his family.

Genesis 37:3-4 *Now Jacob loved Joseph more than any of his other children because Joseph had been born to him in his old age. So one day he gave Joseph a special gift—a beautiful robe. But his brothers hated Joseph because of their father's partiality. They couldn't say a kind word to him.*
A father should impartially love his children.

Ephesians 6:4 *And now a word to you fathers. Don't make your children angry by the way you treat them. Rather, bring them up with the discipline and instruction approved by the Lord.*

Colossians 3:21 *Fathers, don't aggravate your children. If you do, they will become discouraged and quit trying.*

1 Samuel 3:13 *I have warned him continually that judgment is coming for his family, because his sons are blaspheming God and he hasn't disciplined them.*
A father should discipline and instruct his children in love.

What is the role of a woman in her family?

John 16:21 *It will be like a woman experiencing the pains of labor. When her child is born, her anguish gives place to joy because she has brought a new person into the world.*

Genesis 1:28 *God blessed them and told them, "Multiply and fill the earth and subdue it. Be masters over the fish and birds and all the animals."*

Genesis 4:1 *Now Adam slept with his wife, Eve, and she became pregnant. When the time came, she gave birth to Cain, and she said, "With the Lord's help, I have brought forth a man!"*

Genesis 3:20 *Adam named his wife Eve, because she would be the mother of all people everywhere.* God gave women the role of giving birth to the next generation.

Isaiah 49:15 *Can a mother forget her nursing child? Can she feel no love for a child she has borne?*

Isaiah 66:13 *I will comfort you there as a child is comforted by its mother.*

Titus 2:4 *These older women must train the younger women to love their husbands and their children.*
A mother should comfort, love, and nurture her children.

2 Timothy 1:5 *I know that you sincerely trust the Lord, for you have the faith of your mother, Eunice, and your grandmother, Lois.*

2 Timothy 3:15 *You have been taught the holy Scriptures from childhood, and they have given you the wisdom to receive the salvation that comes by trusting in Christ Jesus.*
A mother should have a godly influence in her family.

Proverbs 1:8 *Listen, my child, to what your father teaches you. Don't neglect your mother's teaching.*

Proverbs 23:13 *Don't fail to correct your children. They won't die if you spank them.*

Proverbs 29:15, 17 *To discipline and reprimand a child produces wisdom, but a mother is disgraced by an undisciplined child. . . . Discipline your children, and they will give you happiness and peace of mind.*
A mother has a responsibility to teach and discipline her children.

Proverbs 14:1 *A wise woman builds her house; a foolish woman tears hers down with her own hands.*

Proverbs 31:13-27 *She finds wool and flax and busily spins it. She is like a merchant's ship; she brings her food from afar. She gets up before dawn to prepare breakfast for her household and plan the day's work for her servant girls. She goes out to inspect a field and buys it; with her earnings she plants a vineyard. She is energetic and strong, a hard worker. She watches for bargains; her lights burn late into the night. Her hands are busy spinning thread, her fingers twisting fiber. She extends a helping hand to the poor and opens her arms to the needy. She has no fear of winter for her household because all of them have warm clothes. She quilts her own bedspreads. She dresses like royalty in gowns of finest cloth. Her husband is well known, for he sits in the council meeting with the other civic leaders. She makes belted linen garments and sashes to sell to the merchants. She is clothed with strength and dignity, and she laughs with no fear of the future. When she speaks, her words are wise, and kindness is the rule when she gives instructions. She carefully watches all that goes on in her household and does not have to bear the consequences of laziness.*

The woman should be a diligent worker for her family's good.

PROMISE FROM GOD: Colossians 3:23
Work hard and cheerfully at whatever you do, as though you were working for the Lord rather than for people.

Romance

What does it mean to be romantic?

Song of Songs 7:6, 9 *Oh, how delightful you are, my beloved; how pleasant for utter delight! . . . May your kisses be as exciting as the best wine, smooth and sweet, flowing gently over lips and teeth.*

Song of Songs 4:9 *You have ravished my heart, my treasure, my bride. I am overcome by one glance of your eyes, by a single bead of your necklace.* Romance means enjoying your mate and expressing that enjoyment.

Proverbs 5:18-19 *Let your wife be a fountain of blessing for you. Rejoice in the wife of your youth. She is a loving doe, a graceful deer. Let her breasts satisfy you always. May you always be captivated by her love.* True romance is in finding captivation with your spouse.

Song of Songs 1:2 *Kiss me again and again, for your love is sweeter than wine.*

Song of Songs 2:5-6 *Oh, feed me with your love—your raisins and your apples—for I am utterly lovesick! His left hand is under my head, and his right hand embraces me.*
Romance involves expressing your desire for your mate's affection.

S o n g o f S o n g s 1 : 1 2 - 1 4 *The king is lying on his couch, enchanted by the fragrance of my perfume. My lover is like a sachet of myrrh lying between my breasts. He is like a bouquet of flowers in the gardens of En-gedi.*

S o n g o f S o n g s 2 : 6 *His left hand is under my head, and his right hand embraces me.*
Romance involves physical intimacy.

S o n g o f S o n g s 4 : 1 - 5 *How beautiful you are, my beloved, how beautiful! Your eyes behind your veil are like doves. Your hair falls in waves, like flocks of goats frisking across the slopes of Gilead. Your teeth are as white as sheep, newly shorn and washed. . . . Your lips are like a ribbon of scarlet. Oh, how beautiful your mouth! Your cheeks behind your veil are like pomegranate halves—lovely and delicious. Your neck is as stately as the tower of David, jeweled with the shields of a thousand heroes. Your breasts are like twin fawns of a gazelle, feeding among the lilies.*

S o n g o f S o n g s 4 : 1 0 - 1 1 *How sweet is your love, my treasure, my bride! How much better it is than wine! Your perfume is more fragrant than the richest of spices. Your lips, my bride, are as sweet as honey. Yes, honey and cream are under your tongue. The scent of your clothing is like that of the mountains and the cedars of Lebanon.*

Song of Songs 1:16-17 *What a lovely, pleasant sight you are, my love, as we lie here on the grass, shaded by cedar trees and spreading firs.*
Romance involves expressing how attractive your mate is.

1 Peter 3:3-5 *Don't be concerned about the outward beauty that depends on fancy hairstyles, expensive jewelry, or beautiful clothes. You should be known for the beauty that comes from within, the unfading beauty of a gentle and quiet spirit, which is so precious to God.*
Inner beauty is truly romantic.

1 Peter 3:7-8 *In the same way, you husbands must give honor to your wives. Treat her with understanding as you live together. . . . Be of one mind, full of sympathy toward each other, loving one another with tender hearts and humble minds.*

Philippians 2:3 *Don't be selfish; don't live to make a good impression on others. Be humble, thinking of others as better than yourself.*
Treating your spouse with love and understanding is romantic.

Song of Songs 2:4 *He brings me to the banquet hall, so everyone can see how much he loves me.*

Song of Songs 5:16 *His mouth is altogether sweet; he is lovely in every way. Such, O women of Jerusalem, is my lover, my friend.*

Proverbs 31:28-29 *Her husband praises her: "There are many virtuous and capable women in the world, but you surpass them all!"*
It is romantic to publicly declare your affection for your spouse.

What is the connection between love and romance?

Song of Songs 8:6-7 *Place me like a seal over your heart, or like a seal on your arm. For love is as strong as death, and its jealousy is as enduring as the grave. Love flashes like fire, the brightest kind of flame. Many waters cannot quench love; neither can rivers drown it. If a man tried to buy love with everything he owned, his offer would be utterly despised.*
Love is the source of all true romance.

1 Corinthians 13:4-7 *Love is patient and kind. Love is not jealous or boastful or proud or rude. Love does not demand its own way. Love is not irritable, and it keeps no record of when it has been wronged. It is never glad about injustice but rejoices whenever the truth wins out. Love never gives up, never loses faith, is always hopeful, and endures through every circumstance.*
Love is attractive and romantic.

Why is romance important?

Song of Songs 2:2-3 *Young Man: "Yes, compared to other women, my beloved is like a lily*

267

among thorns." Young Woman: "And compared to other youths, my lover is like the finest apple tree in the orchard. I am seated in his delightful shade, and his fruit is delicious to eat."

Romance expresses the value of both individuals in a loving relationship.

Song of Songs 2:14, 16 *Young Man: "My dove is hiding behind some rocks, behind an outcrop on the cliff. Let me see you; let me hear your voice. For your voice is pleasant, and you are lovely." . . . Young Woman: "My lover is mine, and I am his. He feeds among the lilies!"*

Romance encourages faithfulness.

Song of Songs 4:12-15 *You are like a private garden, my treasure, my bride! You are like a spring that no one else can drink from, a fountain of my own. You are like a lovely orchard bearing precious fruit, with the rarest of perfumes: nard and saffron, calamus and cinnamon, myrrh and aloes, perfume from every incense tree, and every other lovely spice. You are a garden fountain, a well of living water, as refreshing as the streams from the Lebanon mountains.*

Proverbs 5:15-17 *Drink water from your own well—share your love only with your wife. Why spill the water of your springs in public, having sex with just anyone? You should reserve it for yourselves. Don't share it with strangers.*

Romance is a guard for intimacy and faithfulness.

What are the dangers of romance?

Proverbs 6:24-26 *These commands and this teaching will keep you from the immoral woman, from the smooth tongue of an adulterous woman. Don't lust for her beauty. Don't let her coyness seduce you. For a prostitute will bring you to poverty, and sleeping with another man's wife may cost you your very life.*

Proverbs 7:10, 21 *The woman approached him, dressed seductively and sly of heart. . . . So she seduced him with her pretty speech. With her flattery she enticed him.*

Ecclesiastes 7:26 *I discovered that a seductive woman is more bitter than death. Her passion is a trap, and her soft hands will bind you. Those who please God will escape from her, but sinners will be caught in her snare.*

We are to be cautious of whom and what we allow to entertain our affections. Being romanced by anyone other than our lifelong mate can lead to sin and broken relationships.

PROMISE FROM GOD: Jeremiah 31:3 *Long ago the LORD said to Israel: "I have loved you, my people, with an everlasting love. With unfailing love I have drawn you to myself."*

Security

see Insecurity

Self-Control

Why can't we seem to control certain desires?

Galatians 5:24 *Those who belong to Christ Jesus have nailed the passions and desires of their sinful nature to his cross.*
When we don't belong to Christ, our desires will control us.

Romans 12:1 *And so, dear brothers and sisters, I plead with you to give your bodies to God. Let them be a living and holy sacrifice—the kind he will accept.*
We must give ourselves to God and let him change our hearts.

What are some steps to exercising self-control?

Psalm 141:3 *Take control of what I say, O LORD, and keep my lips sealed.*

Romans 13:14 *Let the Lord Jesus Christ take control of you, and don't think of ways to indulge your evil desires.*

2 Peter 1:6 *Knowing God leads to self-control. Self-control leads to patient endurance, and patient endurance leads to godliness.*
The first step in self-control is to let God have control of your heart and life.

Psalm 56:3-4 *When I am afraid, I put my trust in you. O God, I praise your word. I trust in God, so why should I be afraid? What can mere mortals do to me?*

Psalm 61:2 *From the ends of the earth, I will cry to you for help, for my heart is overwhelmed. Lead me to the towering rock of safety.*

1 Corinthians 10:13 *Remember that the temptations that come into your life are no different from what others experience. And God is faithful. He will keep the temptation from becoming so strong that you can't stand up against it. When you are tempted, he will show you a way out so that you will not give in to it.*
God will help us resist temptation if we run to him for help.

Psalm 119:9 *How can a young person stay pure? By obeying your word and following its rules.*

2 Timothy 2:5 *Follow the Lord's rules for doing his work, just as an athlete either follows the rules or is disqualified and wins no prize.*
Self-control involves knowing what you must control. Regular, consistent reading of God's word keeps God's righteous character clearly before us.

Proverbs 13:3 *Those who control their tongue will have a long life; a quick retort can ruin everything.*

Matthew 12:36 *And I tell you this, that you must give account on judgment day of every idle word you speak.*

James 1:26 *If you claim to be religious but don't control your tongue, you are just fooling yourself, and your religion is worthless.*
We exercise self-control by watching what we say. How often we wish we could call back words as soon as they have left our mouth!

PROMISE FROM GOD: 2 Peter 1:6 *Knowing God leads to self-control. Self-control leads to patient endurance, and patient endurance leads to godliness.*

Selfishness

Why is selfishness so destructive?

Genesis 13:10-11 *Lot took a long look at the fertile plains. . . . Lot chose that land for himself.*

Genesis 27:43-44 *"Flee to your uncle Laban in Haran. Stay there with him until your brother's fury is spent."*
Selfishness can destroy relationships—even families.

How can we confront the selfishness in our own lives?

1 John 3:17 *But if one of you has money enough to live well and sees a brother or sister in need and refuses to help—how can God's love be in that person?*
The best cure for the selfish heart is giving.

Philippians 2:4 *Don't think only about your own affairs, but be interested in others, too, and what they are doing.*
Unselfishness is learning to put others first.

PROMISE FROM GOD: Matthew 16:25 *If you try to keep your life for yourself, you will lose it. But if you give up your life for me, you will find true life.*

Selflessness

How does selflessness transform relationships?

Exodus 32:31-32 *So Moses returned to the LORD and said, "Alas, these people have committed a terrible sin. They have made gods of gold for themselves. But now, please forgive their sin—and if not, then blot me out of the record you are keeping."*

1 Chronicles 21:17 *And David said to God, "I am the one who called for the census! I am the one who has sinned and done wrong! But these people are innocent—what have they done? O LORD my God, let your anger fall against me and my family, but do not destroy your people."*
Selflessness can influence others' relationships with God.

1 Corinthians 10:32-33 *Don't give offense to Jews or Gentiles or the church of God. That is the plan I follow, too. I try to please everyone in everything I do. I don't just do what I like or what is best for me, but what is best for them so they may be saved.*

Ruth 1:16 *Ruth replied, "Don't ask me to leave you and turn back. I will go wherever you go and live wherever you live. Your people will be my people, and your God will be my God.*
Selflessness is a willingness to give up our own rights in order to serve others.

Galatians 6:2 *Share each other's troubles and problems, and in this way obey the law of Christ.*

1 Corinthians 10:24 *Don't think only of your own good. Think of other Christians and what is best for them.*
Selflessness helps us think of others' concerns, not just our own.

Genesis 13:8-9 *Then Abram talked it over with Lot. "This arguing between our herdsmen has got to stop," he said. "After all, we are close relatives! I'll tell you what we'll do. Take your choice of any section of the land you want, and we will separate. If you want that area over there, then I'll stay here. If you want to stay in this area, then I'll move on to another place."* Selflessness makes peace with others a greater priority than personal gain.

How can we be more selfless?

Luke 9:23 *Then [Jesus] said to the crowd, "If any of you wants to be my follower, you must put aside your selfish ambition, shoulder your cross daily, and follow me."* Following Jesus requires that we become selfless. As we follow him, selfish ambition will be replaced with selfless devotion.

Galatians 5:22-26 *When the Holy Spirit controls our lives, he will produce this kind of fruit in us: love, joy, peace, patience, kindness, goodness, faithfulness, gentleness, and self-control. . . . Those who belong to Christ Jesus have nailed the passions and desires of their sinful nature to his cross and crucified them there. If we are living now by the Holy Spirit, let us follow the Holy Spirit's leading in every part of our lives. Let us not become conceited, or irritate one another, or be jealous of one another.*

When we come to Christ by faith, we must lay aside our selfish ambition and let the Holy Spirit control our lives. The Holy Spirit's presence helps us to become more self-giving.

John 13:14-15 *Since I, the Lord and Teacher, have washed your feet, you ought to wash each other's feet. I have given you an example to follow. Do as I have done to you.*

Philippians 2:3-5 *Don't be selfish; don't live to make a good impression on others. Be humble, thinking of others as better than yourself. Don't think only about your own affairs, but be interested in others, too, and what they are doing. Your attitude should be the same that Christ Jesus had.*
If we are Jesus' followers, following Jesus' model of servanthood and humility will help us become more selfless.

1 John 3:17 *If one of you has enough money to live well, and sees a brother or sister in need and refuses to help—how can God's love be in that person?*

1 Timothy 6:18 *Tell them to use their money to do good. They should be rich in good works and should give generously to those in need, always being ready to share with others whatever God has given them.*
We should give of ourselves and our resources.

PROMISE FROM GOD: Luke 9:23-24
If any of you wants to be my follower, you must put aside your selfish ambition, shoulder your cross daily, and follow me. If you try to keep your life for yourself, you will lose it. But if you give up your life for me, you will find true life.

Sensitivity

What kind of sensitivity should we try to develop?

Proverbs 28:14 *Blessed are those who have a tender conscience, but the stubborn are headed for serious trouble.*
We need to be sensitive to sin in our own lives and discern what is right and wrong.

Proverbs 27:14 *If you shout a pleasant greeting to your neighbor too early in the morning, it will be counted as a curse!*
We should exercise consideration for and sensitivity to others.

Acts 16:6-10 *Paul and Silas traveled through the area of Phrygia and Galatia, because the Holy Spirit had told them not to go into the province of Asia at that time. Then coming to the borders of Mysia, they headed for the province of Bithynia, but again the Spirit of Jesus did not let them go. So instead, they*

went on through Mysia to the city of Troas. That night Paul had a vision. He saw a man from Macedonia in northern Greece, pleading with him, "Come over here and help us." So we decided to leave for Macedonia at once, for we could only conclude that God was calling us to preach the Good News there.
Christ's followers need to be sensitive to the leading of the Holy Spirit.

Deuteronomy 15:7 *If there are any poor people in your towns when you arrive in the land the LORD your God is giving you, do not be hard-hearted or tightfisted toward them.*
We need to be sensitive to the needs of the poor.

How do we become more thoughtful toward others?

1 Peter 3:8 *All of you should be of one mind, full of sympathy toward each other, loving one another with tender hearts and humble minds.*

Romans 15:1-2 *We may know that these things make no difference, but we cannot just go ahead and do them to please ourselves. We must be considerate of the doubts and fears of those who think these things are wrong. We should please others. If we do what helps them, we will build them up in the Lord.*
We can be thoughtful by considering what will best strengthen another's relationship with God.

Ephesians 5:33 *Each man must love his wife as he loves himself, and the wife must respect her husband.*

Colossians 3:21 *Fathers, don't aggravate your children. If you do, they will become discouraged and quit trying.*

Ephesians 6:1-2 *Children, obey your parents because you belong to the Lord, for this is the right thing to do. "Honor your father and mother." This is the first of the Ten Commandments that ends with a promise.*
We can be thoughtful by obeying God's basic guidelines for family roles and responsibilities—love, respect, and honor.

1 Thessalonians 2:7 *As apostles of Christ we certainly had a right to make some demands of you, but we were as gentle among you as a mother feeding and caring for her own children.*
We can be willing to lay aside our own rights and treat others with gentleness and care.

Proverbs 15:28 *The godly think before speaking.*

James 1:19 *Dear brothers and sisters, be quick to listen, slow to speak, and slow to get angry.*
We can be thoughtful with our words by listening well and thinking before speaking.

Ephesians 4:29 *Don't use foul or abusive language. Let everything you say be good and helpful, so that your words will be an encouragement to those who hear them.*

Proverbs 12:25 *Worry weighs a person down; an encouraging word cheers a person up.*
Our encouraging words can meet another's need.

Romans 12:8 *If your gift is to encourage others, do it! If you have money, share it generously. If God has given you leadership ability, take the responsibility seriously. And if you have a gift for showing kindness to others, do it gladly.*

Hebrews 13:16 *Don't forget to do good and to share what you have with those in need, for such sacrifices are very pleasing to God.*

Proverbs 3:27 *Do not withhold good from those who deserve it when it's in your power to help them.*

Ruth 2:15-16 *When Ruth went back to work again, Boaz ordered his young men, "Let her gather grain right among the sheaves without stopping her. And pull out some heads of barley from the bundles and drop them on purpose for her. Let her pick them up, and don't give her a hard time!"*

Romans 12:13 *When God's children are in need, be the one to help them out. And get into the habit of inviting guests home for dinner or, if they need lodging, for the night.*
God has equipped each of us in special ways to meet the needs of others. When we look for ways to use our gifts for others, we will be more thoughtful toward them and sensitive to their needs.

PROMISE FROM GOD: Ezekiel 11:19
I will give them singleness of heart and put a new spirit within them. I will take away their hearts of stone and give them tender hearts instead.

Separation

What if my spouse and I are currently separated?

Mark 10:7-9 *This explains why a man leaves his father and mother and is joined to his wife, and the two are united into one. Since they are no longer two but one, let no one separate them, for God has joined them together.*

1 Corinthians 7:10-11 *Now, for those who are married I have a command that comes not from me, but from the Lord. A wife must not leave her husband. But if she does leave him, let her remain single or else go back to him. And the husband must not leave his wife.*

Malachi 2:13-16 *You cry out, "Why has the LORD abandoned us?" I'll tell you why! Because the LORD witnessed the vows you and your wife made to each other on your wedding day when you were young. But you have been disloyal to her, though she remained your faithful companion, the wife of your marriage vows. Didn't the LORD make you one with*

*your wife? In body and spirit you are his. . . . So
guard yourself; remain loyal to the wife of your youth.
"For I hate divorce!" says the LORD, the God of Israel.*

1 Corinthians 13:4-5, 7 *Love is patient and
kind. Love is not jealous or boastful or proud or rude.
Love does not demand its own way. Love is not irritable,
and it keeps no record of when it has been wronged. . . .
Love never gives up, never loses faith, is always hopeful,
and endures through every circumstance.*
Our goal during separation should be a loving,
forgiving reunion. God's plan for marriage is for a
man and a woman to experience a loyal, lasting,
loving relationship. His desire is for nothing to
separate the union of marriage.

PROMISE FROM GOD: Romans 8:39
*Nothing in all creation will ever be able to separate us
from the love of God that is revealed in Christ Jesus
our Lord.*

Sex/Sexuality

see also Adultery, Lust, *and* Marriage

In addition to reproduction, what is God's design regarding sex?

Genesis 2:24 *This explains why a man leaves his
father and mother and is joined to his wife and the
two are united into one.*

Proverbs 5:18-19 *Rejoice in the wife of your youth. . . . Let her breasts satisfy you always. May you always be captivated by her love.*

Song of Songs 7:7-8 *You are tall and slim like a palm tree, and your breasts are like its clusters of dates. I said, "I will climb up into the palm tree and take hold of its branches." Now may your breasts be like grape clusters, and the scent of your breath like apples.*

God created sex. Sex is not for reproduction only, but for bonding and enjoyment between husbands and wives. The sexual relationship is a key part of a husband and wife becoming one.

Will God forgive my past sexual sins? Can I truly start over?

Acts 13:38-39 *In this man Jesus there is forgiveness for your sins. Everyone who believes in him is freed from all guilt and declared right with God.*

God will forgive any sexual sin if we turn away from that sin and seek forgiveness.

Romans 1:24 *So God let them go ahead and do whatever shameful things their hearts desired.*

God will not forgive sin when a person persists in that sin. Engaging in persistent, willful sin separates us from God.

How can we fight sexual temptation? It is so powerful in today's world.

1 Corinthians 10:13 *Remember that the temptations that come into your life are no different from what others experience. And God is faithful. He will keep the temptation from becoming so strong that you can't stand up against it.*

We can't fight sexual temptation by ourselves. It is too powerful. Cry out to God to help you. He can and he will.

PROMISE FROM GOD: Hebrews 13:4 *Give honor to marriage, and remain faithful to one another in marriage. God will surely judge people who are immoral and those who commit adultery.*

Sharing

see also Selfishness

In what ways are we expected to share with others?

Galatians 6:2 *Share each other's troubles and problems, and in this way obey the law of Christ.*

Romans 1:11 *I long to visit you so I can share a spiritual blessing with you.*

Proverbs 22:9 *Blessed are those who are generous, because they feed the poor.*

Isaiah 58:7 *I want you to share your food with the hungry and to welcome poor wanderers into your homes. Give clothes to those who need them, and do not hide from relatives who need your help.*

Romans 12:15 *When others are happy, be happy with them. If they are sad, share their sorrow.*

Philippians 1:7 *We have shared together the blessings of God.*
God wants us to share our homes, our resources, our love, our faith, our sympathy, and our joys and sorrows. When we share we connect with others and demonstrate Christ's love.

PROMISE FROM GOD: Matthew 10:42 *If you give even a cup of cold water to one of the least of my followers, you will surely be rewarded.*

Sickness

How does God respond to our sickness?

Psalm 41:3 *The LORD nurses them when they are sick and eases their pain and discomfort.*

Matthew 15:29-31 *A vast crowd brought him the lame, blind, crippled, mute, and many others with physical difficulties, and they laid them before Jesus. And he healed them all. The crowd was amazed! Those who hadn't been able to speak were talking, the crippled were made well, the lame were walking around, and those who had been blind could see again! And they praised the God of Israel.*

Revelation 21:4 *He will remove all of their sorrows, and there will be no more death or sorrow or crying or pain. For the old world and its evils are gone forever.*

Our compassionate, merciful God has full authority over all sickness. He can heal whomever he chooses. We can trust his sovereignty. Eventually, he will remove all sickness and suffering from his people for eternity.

How should we respond in times of personal sickness?

Psalm 103:2-3 *Praise the LORD, I tell myself, and never forget the good things he does for me. He forgives all my sins and heals all my diseases.*
We should praise the Lord for his ability to forgive our sins and heal our diseases. We should praise him even if he chooses not to heal us physically.

James 5:14 *Are any among you sick? They should call for the elders of the church and have them pray over them, anointing them with oil in the name of the Lord.*

2 Corinthians 12:8-10 *Three different times I begged the Lord to take it away. Each time he said, "My gracious favor is all you need. My power works best in your weakness." So now I am glad to boast*

*about my weaknesses, so that the power of Christ may
work through me. Since I know it is all for Christ's
good, I am quite content with my weaknesses and
with insults, hardships, persecutions, and calamities.
For when I am weak, then I am strong.*
We should ask the Lord for healing and be
content with his response.

Psalm 73:26 *My health may fail, and my spirit
may grow weak, but God remains the strength of my
heart; he is mine forever.*

1 Corinthians 15:43 *Our bodies now
disappoint us, but when they are raised, they will be
full of glory. They are weak now, but when they are
raised, they will be full of power.*
Regardless of the condition of our health, we can
rejoice that God remains our strength. Our frail,
earthly bodies will one day be gloriously
transformed for eternity.

How can we minister to the sick?

Psalm 35:13-14 *Yet when they were ill, I
grieved for them. I even fasted and prayed for them,
but my prayers returned unanswered. I was sad, as
though they were my friends or family, as if I were
grieving for my own mother.*

James 5:14-15 *Are any among you sick? They
should call for the elders of the church and have them
pray over them, anointing them with oil in the name*

*of the Lord. And their prayer offered in faith will heal
the sick, and the Lord will make them well. And
anyone who has committed sins will be forgiven.*
We can pray for those who are sick.

John 5:7 *"I can't, sir," the sick man said, "for I
have no one to help me into the pool when the water
is stirred up. While I am trying to get there, someone
else always gets in ahead of me."*

Mark 2:3-5 *Four men arrived carrying a paralyzed
man on a mat. They couldn't get to Jesus through the
crowd, so they dug through the clay roof above his
head. Then they lowered the sick man on his mat,
right down in front of Jesus. Seeing their faith, Jesus
said to the paralyzed man, "My son, your sins are
forgiven."*
We can help the sick gain access to medical care.

Galatians 4:13-14 *Surely you remember that I
was sick when I first brought you the Good News of
Christ. But even though my sickness was revolting to
you, you did not reject me and turn me away. No, you
took me in and cared for me as though I were an
angel from God or even Christ Jesus himself.*

Luke 10:33-34 *Then a despised Samaritan came
along, and when he saw the man, he felt deep pity.
Kneeling beside him, the Samaritan soothed his
wounds with medicine and bandaged them.*

Matthew 25:36 *I was naked, and you gave me clothing. I was sick, and you cared for me. I was in prison, and you visited me.*
We can meet the physical needs of the sick.

PROMISE FROM GOD: Psalm 73:26 *My health may fail, and my spirit may grow weak, but God remains the strength of my heart; he is mine forever.*

Stubbornness

How can we keep from being stubborn?

2 Chronicles 30:8 *Do not be stubborn, as they were, but submit yourselves to the LORD.*
Submit to God in worship and obedience.

Hosea 12:6 *Come back to your God! Act on the principles of love and justice, and always live in confident dependence on your God.*
Return to a life of dependence on God.

Colossians 1:21-22 *You were his enemies, separated from him by your evil thoughts and actions, yet now he has brought you back as his friends. He has done this through his death on the cross in his own human body.*
Christ can remove our spiritual stubbornness and reconcile us to God.

Hebrews 3:13 *You must warn each other every day, as long as it is called "today," so that none of you will be deceived by sin and hardened against God.*
Fellowship with other believers, including exhorting and warning one another, can help preserve us from having hard hearts.

How do we know when we are being stubborn?

Exodus 8:15 *When Pharaoh saw that the frogs were gone, he hardened his heart. He refused to listen to Moses and Aaron, just as the LORD had predicted.*
Stubbornness is refusing to admit the truth in the face of overwhelming evidence.

Proverbs 13:10 *Pride leads to arguments; those who take advice are wise.*
When your position is rooted in pride you are being stubborn.

How do we deal with stubbornness in someone else?

Jonah 2:10 *Then the LORD ordered the fish to spit up Jonah on the beach, and it did.*
God dealt with Jonah's stubbornness with both patience and discipline.

Mark 6:11 *If a village won't welcome you or listen to you, shake off its dust from your feet as you leave. It is a sign that you have abandoned that village to its fate.*

Jesus recognized there are times when we must leave people to the consequences of their own sinful stubbornness.

PROMISE FROM GOD: Jeremiah 32:40 *I will make an everlasting covenant with them, promising not to stop doing good for them. I will put a desire in their hearts to worship me, and they will never leave me.*

Submission

Should we submit to anyone other than the Lord?

Romans 6:13 *Do not let any part of your body become a tool of wickedness, to be used for sinning. Instead, give yourselves completely to God since you have been given new life. And use your whole body as a tool to do what is right for the glory of God.*

Matthew 26:39 *He went on a little farther and fell face down on the ground, praying, "My Father! If it is possible, let this cup of suffering be taken away from me. Yet I want your will, not mine."*
We are to submit our bodies and ourselves to God first of all.

Ephesians 5:21 *Submit to one another out of reverence for Christ.*
Christians are to submit to one another.

1 Peter 5:5 *You younger men, accept the authority of the elders. And all of you, serve each other in humility, for "God sets himself against the proud, but he shows favor to the humble."*
We should submit to those in authority over us.

Ephesians 5:22 *You wives will submit to your husbands as you do to the Lord.*
A Christian wife should submit to her husband.

Ephesians 5:25, 28 *You husbands must love your wives with the same love Christ showed the church. . . . Husbands ought to love their wives as they love their own bodies.*
A Christian husband should submit to Christ in relating to his wife.

Ephesians 6:1 *Children, obey your parents because you belong to the Lord, for this is the right thing to do.*
Children should submit to their parents.

Ephesians 6:4 *Don't make your children angry by the way you treat them. Rather, bring them up with the discipline and instruction approved by the Lord.*
Christian parents should submit to Christ in relating to their children.

Ephesians 6:5 *Slaves, obey your earthly masters with deep respect and fear. Serve them sincerely as you would serve Christ.*
Employees should submit to their employers.

Ephesians 6:9 *You masters must treat your slaves right. Don't threaten them; remember, you both have the same Master in heaven, and he has no favorites.*
Christian employers should submit to Christ in relating to their employees.

Romans 13:1-2 *Obey the government, for God is the one who put it there. All governments have been placed in power by God. So those who refuse to obey the laws of the land are refusing to obey God, and punishment will follow.*
We should submit to the government.

How should we submit?

Ephesians 5:21 *You will submit to one another out of reverence for Christ.*
When we submit to the authority of another human being, we should do it primarily out of reverence for Christ.

Hebrews 12:9 *Since we respect our earthly fathers who disciplined us, should we not all the more cheerfully submit to the discipline of our heavenly Father and live forever?*
We are to submit to authority and discipline cheerfully, even when it is unpleasant.

Hebrews 13:17 *Obey your spiritual leaders and do what they say. Their work is to watch over your souls, and they know they are accountable to God.*

Give them reason to do this joyfully and not with sorrow. That would certainly not be for your benefit.
We are to submit to spiritual leaders with thankfulness, realizing that their instruction is for our good.

PROMISE FROM GOD: Proverbs 29:18 *When people do not accept divine guidance, they run wild. But whoever obeys the law is happy.*

Success

What is true success in God's eyes?

Ecclesiastes 12:13 *Fear God and obey his commands, for this is the duty of every person. God will judge us for everything we do, including every secret thing, whether good or bad.*
True success is living a life of obedience to God and doing what is right.

Acts 16:31 *Believe on the Lord Jesus and you will be saved.*
True success is based on our belief in Jesus.

Matthew 20:26 *Among you it should be quite different. Whoever wants to be a leader among you must be your servant.*
God has a different definition of success than the world. For him, serving and helping others is one of life's greatest achievements.

Is it OK to try to be successful in this life?

Proverbs 16:3 *Commit your work to the LORD, and then your plans will succeed.*
Earthly success is a worthwhile goal, but commitment to God is even more worthwhile. Only when our work is done from a position of commitment to God can we consider ourselves to be truly successful.

Proverbs 12:24 *Work hard and become a leader; be lazy and become a slave.*

Proverbs 22:29 *Do you see any truly competent workers? They will serve kings rather than ordinary people.*
Working hard, having integrity, being committed, serving others, and planning are all important positive character traits, and they are naturally rewarded with success in the world.

Genesis 39:2-3 *The LORD was with Joseph and blessed him greatly as he served in the home of his Egyptian master . . . giving him success in everything he did.*

Exodus 33:14 *The LORD replied, "I will personally go with you. . . . Everything will be fine for you."*
God enjoys giving his people material blessing, but he urges them never to sacrifice spiritual health for worldly wealth.

PROMISE FROM GOD: Psalm 84:11
The LORD God is our light and protector. He gives us grace and glory. No good thing will the LORD withhold from those who do what is right.

Support

How can I support my spouse?

Matthew 19:4-6 *"Haven't you read the Scriptures?" Jesus replied. "They record that from the beginning 'God made them male and female.' And he said, 'This explains why a man leaves his father and mother and is joined to his wife, and the two are united into one.' Since they are no longer two but one, let no one separate them, for God has joined them together."*

Ecclesiastes 4:9-10 *Two people can accomplish more than twice as much as one; they get a better return for their labor. If one person falls, the other can reach out and help. But people who are alone when they fall are in real trouble.*
I can support my spouse through the unity of our marriage relationship.

Genesis 2:18 *The LORD God said, "It is not good for the man to be alone. I will make a companion who will help him."*

Proverbs 31:11-12 *Her husband can trust her, and she will greatly enrich his life. She will not hinder him but help him all her life.*
A wife can support her husband by being a helpful, trustworthy, lifelong companion.

Proverbs 31:28-31 *Her children stand and bless her. Her husband praises her: "There are many virtuous and capable women in the world, but you surpass them all!" Charm is deceptive, and beauty does not last; but a woman who fears the LORD will be greatly praised. Reward her for all she has done. Let her deeds publicly declare her praise.*
A husband can support his wife by valuing, respecting, and praising her.

Genesis 24:67 *And Isaac brought Rebekah into his mother's tent, and she became his wife. He loved her very much, and she was a special comfort to him after the death of his mother.*

2 Samuel 12:24 *Then David comforted Bathsheba, his wife, and slept with her. She became pregnant and gave birth to a son, and they named him Solomon. The LORD loved the child.*
I can comfort my spouse.

How can we support others?

Proverbs 27:10 *Never abandon a friend—either yours or your father's. Then in your time of need, you won't have to ask your relatives for assistance.*

We can support others by being a faithful friend.

Hebrews 12:15 *Look after each other so that none of you will miss out on the special favor of God. Watch out that no bitter root of unbelief rises up among you, for whenever it springs up, many are corrupted by its poison.*
We can support others by being involved in and concerned about their lives.

1 Peter 3:8 *Finally, all of you should be of one mind, full of sympathy toward each other, loving one another with tender hearts and humble minds.*
We can support others by being sympathetic, loving, and humble.

James 5:16 *Confess your sins to each other and pray for each other so that you may be healed. The earnest prayer of a righteous person has great power and wonderful results.*
We can support others in prayer.

Psalm 69:20 *If only one person would show some pity; if only one would turn and comfort me.*

Job 42:11 *They consoled him and comforted him because of all the trials the LORD had brought against him.*

2 Corinthians 1:4 *He comforts us in all our troubles so that we can comfort others. When others are troubled, we will be able to give them the same comfort God has given us.*

1 Thessalonians 3:7 *So we have been greatly comforted, dear brothers and sisters, in all of our own crushing troubles and suffering, because you have remained strong in your faith.*
We can support others by comforting them.

1 Samuel 23:16 *Jonathan went to find David and encouraged him to stay strong in his faith in God.*

Acts 14:22 *They strengthened the believers. They encouraged them to continue in the faith, reminding them that they must enter into the Kingdom of God through many tribulations.*

1 Thessalonians 5:11 *Encourage each other and build each other up, just as you are already doing.*
We can support others with our encouragement.

Romans 12:13 *When God's children are in need, be the one to help them out. And get into the habit of inviting guests home for dinner or, if they need lodging, for the night.*

2 Corinthians 8:14 *Right now you have plenty and can help them. Then at some other time they can share with you when you need it. In this way, everyone's needs will be met.*
We can support others by meeting their practical needs.

PROMISE FROM GOD: Isaiah 46:4 *I will be your God throughout your lifetime—until your hair is white with age. I made you, and I will care for you. I will carry you along and save you.*

Sympathy

see **Empathy**

Talk

see **Communication**

Teamwork

What are some of the keys to successful teamwork?

Amos 3:3 *Can two people walk together without agreeing on the direction?*

Nehemiah 2:17-18 *But now I said to them, "You know full well the tragedy of our city. It lies in ruins, and its gates are burned. Let us rebuild the wall of Jerusalem and rid ourselves of this disgrace!" Then I told them about how the gracious hand of God had been on me, and about my conversation with the king. They replied at once, "Good! Let's rebuild the wall!" So they began the good work.*

Clear vision and goals are keys to successful teamwork.

1 Corinthians 1:10 *Let there be real harmony so there won't be divisions in the church. I plead with you to be of one mind, united in thought and purpose.*

Philippians 2:1-2 *Is there any encouragement from belonging to Christ? Any comfort from his love? Any fellowship together in the Spirit? Are your hearts tender and sympathetic? Then make me truly happy by agreeing wholeheartedly with each other, loving one another, and working together with one heart and purpose.*
Harmony and unity help us work together.

Ezra 3:8 *The construction of the Temple of God began in midspring, during the second year after they arrived in Jerusalem. The work force was made up of everyone who had returned from exile.*

Nehemiah 4:6 *At last the wall was completed to half its original height around the entire city, for the people had worked very hard.*

Luke 5:18-20 *Some men came carrying a paralyzed man on a sleeping mat. They tried to push through the crowd to Jesus, but they couldn't reach him. So they went up to the roof, took off some tiles, and lowered the sick man down into the crowd, still on his mat, right in front of Jesus. Seeing their faith, Jesus said to the man, "Son, your sins are forgiven."*
Determination and hard work help us succeed together.

Nehemiah 4:16, 21 *From then on, only half my men worked while the other half stood guard with spears, shields, bows, and coats of mail. . . . We worked early and late, from sunrise to sunset. And half the men were always on guard.*
Teamwork involves cooperation.

1 Corinthians 12:7, 25 *A spiritual gift is given to each of us as a means of helping the entire church. . . . This makes for harmony among the members, so that all the members care for each other equally.*

Romans 12:4-5 *Just as our bodies have many parts and each part has a special function, so it is with Christ's body. We are all parts of his one body, and each of us has different work to do. And since we are all one body in Christ, we belong to each other, and each of us needs all the others.*

1 Corinthians 12:27 *Now all of you together are Christ's body, and each one of you is a separate and necessary part of it.*
Teamwork means using our gifts to fulfill our role and encouraging others to use their gifts to fulfill their role.

Exodus 4:15-16 *You will talk to him, giving him the words to say. I will help both of you to speak clearly, and I will tell you what to do. Aaron will be your spokesman to the people, and you will be as God to him, telling him what to say.*

Exodus 17:12-13 *Moses' arms finally became too tired to hold up the staff any longer. So Aaron and Hur found a stone for him to sit on. Then they stood on each side, holding up his hands until sunset. As a result, Joshua and his troops were able to crush the army of Amalek.*

Teamwork means helping each other finish the job.

How do we team up with God in his work?

John 15:5 *Yes, I am the vine; you are the branches. Those who remain in me, and I in them, will produce much fruit. For apart from me you can do nothing.*

We should recognize our dependency on God.

Matthew 6:10 *May your Kingdom come soon. May your will be done here on earth, just as it is in heaven.*

Romans 12:2 *Don't copy the behavior and customs of this world, but let God transform you into a new person by changing the way you think. Then you will know what God wants you to do, and you will know how good and pleasing and perfect his will really is.*

We should align ourselves with God's will.

John 5:19 *Jesus replied, "I assure you, the Son can do nothing by himself. He does only what he sees the Father doing. Whatever the Father does, the Son also does."*

We are to be attentive to what God is doing and join him in his work.

Jonah 3:1-3 *Then the LORD spoke to Jonah a second time: "Get up and go to the great city of Nineveh, and deliver the message of judgment I have given you." This time Jonah obeyed the Lord's command and went to Nineveh.*

John 14:23 *Jesus replied, "All those who love me will do what I say. My Father will love them, and we will come to them and live with them."*
We should be obedient to what God tells us to do.

PROMISE FROM GOD:
Ecclesiastes 4:9, 12 *Two people can accomplish more than twice as much as one; they get a better return for their labor. . . . Three are even better, for a triple-braided cord is not easily broken.*

Temper

see also Anger

How does one's short temper affect relationships?

1 Samuel 25:17 *You'd better think fast, for there is going to be trouble for our master and his whole family. He's so ill-tempered that no one can even talk to him!*

James 1:19-20 *Dear brothers and sisters, be quick to listen, slow to speak, and slow to get angry. Your anger can never make things right in God's sight.*

James 3:5 *So also, the tongue is a small thing, but what enormous damage it can do. A tiny spark can set a great forest on fire.*
A short temper causes a great deal of damage to ourselves and to others.

Proverbs 22:24-25 *Keep away from angry, short-tempered people, or you will learn to be like them and endanger your soul.*
Short tempers are contagious. Those who are close to us will either join in or distance themselves from us.

How can we better control our tempers?

Galatians 5:16-18, 22-23 *I advise you to live according to your new life in the Holy Spirit. Then you won't be doing what your sinful nature craves. The old sinful nature loves to do evil, which is just opposite from what the Holy Spirit wants. And the Spirit gives us desires that are opposite from what the sinful nature desires. These two forces are constantly fighting each other, and your choices are never free from this conflict. But when you are directed by the Holy Spirit, you are no longer subject to the law. . . . But when the Holy Spirit controls our lives, he will produce this kind of fruit in us: love, joy, peace, patience, kindness, goodness, faithfulness, gentleness, and self-control. Here there is no conflict with the law.*

P r o v e r b s 1 6 : 3 2 *It is better to be patient than powerful; it is better to have self-control than to conquer a city.*

C o l o s s i a n s 3 : 8 - 1 0 *But now is the time to get rid of anger, rage, malicious behavior, slander, and dirty language. . . . In its place you have clothed yourselves with a brand-new nature that is continually being renewed as you learn more and more about Christ, who created this new nature within you.* God is even-tempered. As we get to know God and live in his Spirit, we recognize the value of having an even temper. We model Jesus' earthly example through our new nature.

E p h e s i a n s 4 : 2 , 2 6 - 2 7 *Be humble and gentle. Be patient with each other, making allowance for each other's faults because of your love. . . . And "don't sin by letting anger gain control over you." Don't let the sun go down while you are still angry, for anger gives a mighty foothold to the Devil.*

J a m e s 3 : 1 7 *The wisdom that comes from heaven is first of all pure. It is also peace loving, gentle at all times, and willing to yield to others. It is full of mercy and good deeds. It shows no partiality and is always sincere.*

As we rid ourselves of our old nature, we treat others differently. Our new, even-tempered nature offers humility, gentleness, patience, forgiveness, love, peace, mercy, sincerity, and kindness to others.

Proverbs 19:11 *People with good sense restrain their anger; they earn esteem by overlooking wrongs.*

Proverbs 29:11 *A fool gives full vent to anger, but a wise person quietly holds it back.*
Remain calm and do not be controlled by anger.

James 1:19-20 *Dear brothers and sisters, be quick to listen, slow to speak, and slow to get angry. Your anger can never make things right in God's sight.*

Proverbs 17:27 *A truly wise person uses few words; a person with understanding is even-tempered.*

Proverbs 15:1 *A gentle answer turns away wrath, but harsh words stir up anger.*
Think with understanding before speaking, and use few and gentle words.

Proverbs 22:24-25 *Keep away from angry, short-tempered people, or you will learn to be like them and endanger your soul.*
Avoid other short-tempered people.

PROMISE FROM GOD: Psalm 103:8 *The LORD is merciful and gracious; he is slow to get angry and full of unfailing love.*

Thoughtfulness

see Sensitivity

Touch

How did Jesus use physical touch during his time on earth?

Mark 10:16 *He took the children into his arms and placed his hands on their heads and blessed them.*

Luke 4:40 *As the sun went down that evening, people throughout the village brought sick family members to Jesus. No matter what their diseases were, the touch of his hand healed every one.*

Mark 5:28 *She thought to herself, "If I can just touch his clothing, I will be healed."*

John 20:27 *He said to Thomas, "Put your finger here and see my hands. Put your hand into the wound in my side. Don't be faithless any longer. Believe!"*
Jesus used touch to comfort, affirm, heal, bless, and encourage.

What are some of the good uses of physical touch?

Genesis 33:4 *Then Esau ran to meet him and embraced him affectionately and kissed him. Both of them were in tears.*

Luke 15:20 *He returned home to his father. And while he was still a long distance away, his father saw him coming. Filled with love and compassion, he ran to his son, embraced him, and kissed him.*
Physical touch is used for greetings.

1 Samuel 20:41 *As soon as the boy was gone, David came out from where he had been hiding near the stone pile. Then David bowed to Jonathan with his face to the ground. Both of them were in tears as they embraced each other and said good-bye, especially David.*

Acts 20:37 *They wept aloud as they embraced him in farewell.*
Physical touch is used to say good-bye.

Luke 7:38 *Then she knelt behind him at his feet, weeping. Her tears fell on his feet, and she wiped them off with her hair. Then she kept kissing his feet and putting perfume on them.*
Physical touch can be used to say thank you.

Song of Songs 1:2 *Young Woman: "Kiss me again and again, for your love is sweeter than wine."*

Song of Songs 2:6 *His left hand is under my head, and his right hand embraces me.*
Physical touch is a part of intimacy in marriage.

Acts 6:6 *These seven were presented to the apostles, who prayed for them as they laid their hands on them.*

Acts 8:17 *Then Peter and John laid their hands upon these believers, and they received the Holy Spirit.*

1 Timothy 4:14 *Do not neglect the spiritual gift you received through the prophecies spoken to you when the elders of the church laid their hands on you.*
Physical touch is part of ministry.

What are some of the abuses of physical touch?

Exodus 21:12 *Anyone who hits a person hard enough to cause death must be put to death.*

John 19:3 *"Hail! King of the Jews!" they mocked, and they hit him with their fists.*

Job 31:21-22 *If my arm has abused an orphan because I thought I could get away with it, then let my shoulder be wrenched out of place! Let my arm be torn from its socket!*
Physical touch shouldn't be used for violence.

Luke 22:47-48 *Even as he said this, a mob approached, led by Judas, one of his twelve disciples. Judas walked over to Jesus and greeted him with a kiss. But Jesus said, "Judas, how can you betray me, the Son of Man, with a kiss?"*
Physical touch shouldn't be used to deceive.

Proverbs 6:29 *So it is with the man who sleeps with another man's wife. He who embraces her will not go unpunished.*

Leviticus 18:6 *You must never have sexual intercourse with a close relative, for I am the LORD.*

Romans 1:26-27 *That is why God abandoned them to their shameful desires. Even the women turned against the natural way to have sex and instead indulged in sex with each other. And the men, instead of having normal sexual relationships with women, burned with lust for each other. Men did shameful things with other men and, as a result, suffered within themselves the penalty they so richly deserved.*

Sexual sins involve abusing the gift of physical touch.

PROMISE FROM GOD: John 20:27 *[Jesus] said to Thomas, "Put your finger here and see my hands. Put your hand into the wound in my side. Don't be faithless any longer. Believe!"*

Trust

How can we be trustworthy?

Proverbs 12:17 *An honest witness tells the truth; a false witness tells lies.*

Zechariah 8:16 *This is what you must do: Tell the truth to each other. Render verdicts in your courts that are just and that lead to peace.*

Ephesians 4:25 *Put away all falsehood and "tell your neighbor the truth" because we belong to each other.*

Proverbs 11:3 *Good people are guided by their honesty; treacherous people are destroyed by their dishonesty.*
Be truthful and honest.

Matthew 25:20-21 *The servant to whom he had entrusted the five bags of gold said, "Sir, you gave me five bags of gold to invest, and I have doubled the amount." The master was full of praise. "Well done, my good and faithful servant. You have been faithful in handling this small amount, so now I will give you many more responsibilities. Let's celebrate together!"*

Daniel 6:4 *The other administrators and princes began searching for some fault in the way Daniel was handling his affairs, but they couldn't find anything to criticize. He was faithful and honest and always responsible.*

2 Kings 12:15 *No accounting was required from the construction supervisors, because they were honest and faithful workers.*
Be faithful and responsible.

Numbers 30:2 *A man who makes a vow to the LORD or makes a pledge under oath must never break it. He must do exactly what he said he would do.*
Do exactly what you say you will do.

Deuteronomy 25:13 *You must use accurate scales when you weigh out merchandise.*

Proverbs 11:1 *The LORD hates cheating, but he delights in honesty.*

Proverbs 20:23 *The LORD despises double standards; he is not pleased by dishonest scales.*

Hosea 12:7 *The people are like crafty merchants selling from dishonest scales—they love to cheat.*
Be fair in your dealings with others.

Proverbs 11:13 *A gossip goes around revealing secrets, but those who are trustworthy can keep a confidence.*
Keep confidences.

PROMISE FROM GOD: Hebrews 10:23 *God can be trusted to keep his promise.*

Unity

What is true unity?

1 Corinthians 12:18-20 *God made our bodies with many parts, and he has put each part just where he wants it. What a strange thing a body would be if it had only one part! Yes, there are many parts, but only one body.*

Romans 12:4-5 *Just as our bodies have many parts and each part has a special function, so it is with Christ's body. We are all parts of his one body, and each of us has different work to do. And since we are all one body in Christ, we belong to each other, and each of us needs all the others.*

Galatians 3:28 *There is no longer Jew or Gentile, slave or free, male or female. For you are all Christians—you are one in Christ Jesus.*
Unity is not the same as uniformity. We all have unique gifts and personalities. True unity allows us to celebrate and appreciate our differences while reaching the common goal of serving our Lord.

In addition to the church, what are some areas of our lives in which unity is important?

Ephesians 5:31 *As the Scriptures say, "A man leaves his father and mother and is joined to his wife, and the two are united into one."*

Genesis 13:8 *Then Abram talked it over with Lot. "This arguing between our herdsmen has got to stop," he said. "After all, we are close relatives!"*

1 Samuel 18:1, 3 *After David had finished talking with Saul, he met Jonathan, the king's son. There was an immediate bond of love between them, and they became the best of friends. . . . And Jonathan made a special vow to be David's friend.*

We should have unity in our marriage, in our family, and in our friendships.

How do we achieve unity?

Romans 15:5 *May God, who gives this patience and encouragement, help you live in complete harmony with each other—each with the attitude of Christ Jesus toward the other.*
Unity comes when we adopt a Christlike attitude.

Ephesians 4:11-13 *Their responsibility is to equip God's people to do his work and build up the church, the body of Christ, until we come to such unity in our faith and knowledge of God's Son that we will be mature and full grown in the Lord, measuring up to the full stature of Christ.*
Unity comes when we exercise our God-given gifts to build one another up.

Ephesians 4:2-3 *Be humble and gentle. Be patient with each other, making allowance for each other's faults because of your love. Always keep yourselves united in the Holy Spirit, and bind yourselves together with peace.*

1 Peter 3:8 *Finally, all of you should be of one mind, full of sympathy toward each other, loving one another with tender hearts and humble minds.*
Unity comes when we have sympathy, humility, and love for each other.

Colossians 3:13-14 *You must make allowance for each other's faults and forgive the person who offends you. . . . Love is what binds us all together in perfect harmony.*
Unity comes when we forgive each other.

PROMISE FROM GOD: Romans 15:6 *Then all of you can join together with one voice, giving praise and glory to God, the Father of our Lord Jesus Christ.*

Used/Using Others/ Feeling Used

How can we avoid taking advantage of others?

Nehemiah 5:15 *This was quite a contrast to the former governors who had laid heavy burdens on the people, demanding a daily ration of food and wine, besides a pound of silver. Even their assistants took advantage of the people. But because of my fear of God, I did not act that way.*

Deuteronomy 24:10 *If you lend anything to your neighbor, do not enter your neighbor's house to claim the security.*
Realize that God will hold us accountable for the way we treat others.

Genesis 16:1-3 *Sarai, Abram's wife, had no children. So Sarai took her servant, an Egyptian woman named Hagar, and gave her to Abram so she could bear his children. "The LORD has kept me from having any children," Sarai said to Abram. "Go and sleep with my servant. Perhaps I can have children through her." And Abram agreed. So Sarai, Abram's wife, took Hagar the Egyptian servant and gave her to Abram as a wife.*

Realize that God can accomplish his purposes without our having to use other people.

How can we avoid being used by others?

Proverbs 23:1 *When dining with a ruler, pay attention to what is put before you.*

Isaiah 39:1-2 *Hezekiah welcomed the Babylonian envoys and showed them everything in his treasure-houses. . . . He also took them to see his armory and showed them all his other treasures—everything! There was nothing in his palace or kingdom that Hezekiah did not show them.*

Jude 1:16 *These people are grumblers and complainers, doing whatever evil they feel like. They are loudmouthed braggarts, and they flatter others to get favors in return.*

Don't be vulnerable; be alert, aware, and knowledgeable.

How should we respond to those who abuse us or others?

Genesis 29:15-30 *Laban said to him, "You shouldn't work for me without pay just because we are relatives. How much do you want?" . . . Since Jacob was in love with Rachel, he told her father, "I'll work for you seven years if you'll give me Rachel, your younger daughter, as my wife." . . . Finally, the time came for him to marry her. "I have fulfilled my contract," Jacob said to Laban. "Now give me my wife so we can be married." . . . That night, when it was dark, Laban took Leah to Jacob, and he slept with her. . . . But when Jacob woke up in the morning—it was Leah! "What sort of trick is this?" Jacob raged at Laban. "I worked seven years for Rachel. What do you mean by this trickery?" . . . "Wait until the bridal week is over, and you can have Rachel, too—that is, if you promise to work another seven years for me." . . . So Jacob slept with Rachel, too, and he loved her more than Leah. He then stayed and worked the additional seven years.*

We should respond with integrity regardless of the way others treat us.

Luke 16:2 *His employer called him in and said, "What's this I hear about your stealing from me? Get your report in order, because you are going to be dismissed."*

1 Corinthians 5:11 *You are not to associate with anyone who claims to be a Christian yet indulges in sexual sin, or is greedy, or worships idols, or is abusive, or a drunkard, or a swindler. Don't even eat with such people.*
Sometimes we need to take action against injustice, sometimes we need to accept injustice, and sometimes we need to stop associating with unjust people.

PROMISE FROM GOD: Leviticus 25:17 *Show your fear of God by not taking advantage of each other. I, the LORD, am your God.*

Vulnerability

Are there ways in which we should be vulnerable?

Psalm 139.23-24 *Search me, O God, and know my heart; test me and know my thoughts. Point out anything in me that offends you, and lead me along the path of everlasting life.*

Hebrews 4:12-13 *The word of God is full of living power. It is sharper than the sharpest knife, cutting deep into our innermost thoughts and desires. It exposes us for what we really are. Nothing in all creation can hide from him. Everything is naked and*

*exposed before his eyes. This is the God to whom we
must explain all that we have done.*
We should open our hearts and lives fully to God
and let him do his work in us.

Hebrews 10:33 *Sometimes you were exposed to
public ridicule and were beaten, and sometimes you
helped others who were suffering the same things.*

Matthew 5:11-12 *God blesses you when you are
mocked and persecuted and lied about because you are
my followers. Be happy about it! Be very glad! For a
great reward awaits you in heaven. And remember,
the ancient prophets were persecuted, too.*
We should be willing to suffer humiliation and
shame for Christ.

Genesis 2:25 *Although Adam and his wife were
both naked, neither of them felt any shame.*
We should be vulnerable to our mate.

How should we treat those who are vulnerable?

Genesis 9:22-23 *Ham, the father of Canaan,
saw that his father was naked and went outside and
told his brothers. Shem and Japheth took a robe, held
it over their shoulders, walked backward into the tent,
and covered their father's naked body. As they did
this, they looked the other way so they wouldn't see
him naked.*

Proverbs 23:10 *Don't steal the land of defenseless orphans by moving the ancient boundary markers.*
We should do what we can to "cover" those who are vulnerable, and we should not take advantage of their vulnerability.

Job 6:14 *One should be kind to a fainting friend.*

Isaiah 58:7 *I want you to share your food with the hungry and to welcome poor wanderers into your homes. Give clothes to those who need them, and do not hide from relatives who need your help.*
We should help those who are vulnerable and treat them with mercy, compassion, and kindness.

Psalm 82:4 *Rescue the poor and helpless; deliver them from the grasp of evil people.*

Proverbs 31:9 *Yes, speak up for the poor and helpless, and see that they get justice.*
God wants us to protect the vulnerable so others will not take advantage of them.

PROMISES FROM GOD: Psalm 12:5 *I have seen violence done to the helpless, and I have heard the groans of the poor. Now I will rise up to rescue them, as they have longed for me to do.*

Romans 5:6 *When we were utterly helpless, Christ came at just the right time and died for us sinners.*

Wives

How should a wife treat her husband?

Proverbs 31:11-12 *Her husband can trust her, and she will greatly enrich his life. She will not hinder him but help him all her life.*

Ephesians 5:22-24 *You wives will submit to your husbands as you do to the Lord. For a husband is the head of his wife as Christ is the head of his body, the church; he gave his life to be her Savior. As the church submits to Christ, so you wives must submit to your husbands in everything.*
A wife should love her husband sacrificially, help and support him, believe in him, and submit to him as he submits to Christ.

How does God want men to treat their wives?

Ephesians 5:25, 28-29, 33 *You husbands must love your wives with the same love Christ showed the church. . . . Husbands ought to love their wives as they love their own bodies. . . . No one hates his own body but lovingly cares for it. . . . Each man must love his wife as he loves himself.*

Colossians 3:19 *You husbands must love your wives and never treat them harshly.*
A husband must love his wife with sacrificial love and treat her with gentleness and kindness.

Proverbs 18:22 *The man who finds a wife finds a treasure and receives favor from the LORD.*
A husband should treat his wife as the treasure that she really is.

Genesis 2:23 *"At last!" Adam exclaimed. "She is part of my own flesh and bone! She will be called 'woman,' because she was taken out of a man."*
A husband should always maintain an appreciative attitude toward his wife.

1 Corinthians 7:3, 5 *The husband should not deprive his wife of sexual intimacy, which is her right as a married woman, nor should the wife deprive her husband. . . . So do not deprive each other of sexual relations.*
A husband should give his wife sexual intimacy and not withhold it.

1 Corinthians 7:32-33 *An unmarried man can spend his time doing the Lord's work and thinking how to please him. But a married man can't do that so well. He has to think about his earthly responsibilities and how to please his wife.*
A husband must forego some of his own plans in order to take care of his wife and please her.

Ephesians 5:23 *A husband is the head of his wife as Christ is the head of his body, the church; he gave his life to be her Savior.*
In the marriage relationship a husband needs to exercise responsibility and leadership—even give his life for his wife.

1 Peter 3:7 *In the same way, you husbands must give honor to your wives. Treat her with understanding as you live together. She may be weaker than you are, but she is your equal partner in God's gift of new life.*
A husband must treat his wife with honor and understanding.

PROMISE FROM GOD: Psalm 128:3-4 *Your wife will be like a fruitful vine, flourishing within your home. . . . That is the LORD's reward for those who fear him.*

Words

see **Communication**

Worth/Worthiness

Of what is God worthy?

Psalm 29:1-2 *Give honor to the LORD, you angels; give honor to the LORD for his glory and strength. Give honor to the LORD for the glory of his name. Worship the LORD in the splendor of his holiness.*

Psalm 145:3 *Great is the LORD! He is most worthy of praise! His greatness is beyond discovery!*

2 Samuel 22:4 *I will call on the LORD, who is worthy of praise, for he saves me from my enemies.*

Psalm 33:4 *The word of the LORD holds true, and everything he does is worthy of our trust.*
God is worthy of our praise, worship, reverence, and trust.

What are we worth—what is our value to God?

Psalm 8:5 *You made us only a little lower than God, and you crowned us with glory and honor.*

Deuteronomy 26:18 *The LORD has declared today that you are his people, his own special treasure, just as he promised, and that you must obey all his commands.*

1 Corinthians 6:20 *God bought you with a high price. So you must honor God with your body.*

Ephesians 1:4-7 *Long ago, even before he made the world, God loved us and chose us in Christ to be holy and without fault in his eyes.*
God made us in his own image, and he values us highly! He also emphasizes how important our souls are to him. Before God made the world he chose us to be born as his unique creations.

What does God consider worthwhile?

1 Corinthians 13:13 *There are three things that will endure—faith, hope, and love—and the greatest of these is love.*

Faith, hope, and love are worthwhile to God.

Proverbs 4:7 *Getting wisdom is the most important thing you can do! And whatever else you do, get good judgment.*
Wisdom and good judgment are worthwhile to God.

Ecclesiastes 7:1 *A good reputation is more valuable than the most expensive perfume.*
A good reputation is worthwhile to God.

Proverbs 20:15 *Wise speech is rarer and more valuable than gold and rubies.*
Wise and helpful words are worthwhile to God.

Proverbs 31:10 *Who can find a virtuous and capable wife? She is worth more than precious rubies.*
Virtue and exemplary conduct are worthwhile to God.

PROMISE FROM GOD: Psalm 8:5 *For you made us only a little lower than God, and you crowned us with glory and honor.*

INDEX